Key Words for Fluency

Pre-intermediate
collocation practice

learning and practising the
most useful words of English

George Woolard

THOMSON™

United Kingdom • United States • Australia • Canad

THOMSON

Key Words for Fluency
Pre-intermediate

George Woolard

Publisher: Christopher Wenger

Director of Product Development:
Anita Raducanu

Director of Product Marketing: Amy Mabley

Development Editor: Jimmie Hill

Production Manager: Sally Giangrande

Intl. Marketing Manager: Ian Martin

Sr. Print Buyer: Mary Beth Hennebury

Illustrator: Anna Macleod

Cover/Text Designer: Anna Macleod

Cover Image: © Anna Macleod

Printer: Canale

Printed in Italy.

1 2 3 4 5 6 7 8 9 10   09 08 07 06 05

For more information, contact Thomson Learning, High Holborn House, 50/51 Bedford Row, London WC1R 4LR, United Kingdom, or Thomson Heinle, 25 Thomson Place, Boston, MA 02210 USA, or you can visit our internet site at elt.thomson.com

For permission to use material from this book, submit a request online at www.thomsonrights.com

ISBN: 0-7593-9629-9

The author

George Woolard is an experienced ELT teacher and trainer who has worked in Greece, Malaysia and the UK. He now teaches at Stevenson College, Edinburgh. His publications include **Lessons with Laughter** and **Grammar with Laughter** *(Thomson ELT)*.

Acknowledgements

I am grateful to Michael Lewis for his comments in the early stages of the development of the Key Word approach that underpins this book. I should also like to thank those colleagues and students at Stevenson College, Edinburgh, whose feedback proved invaluable during the development and writing of this material.
Lastly, I am particularly grateful to my editor, Jimmie Hill, for his meticulous comments and guidance in shaping this book.

George Woolard

To the student

Dear Student

Words have friends!

A lot of students think that learning vocabulary is just learning more new words. However, it is not enough to know only a word and its meaning. You also need to know what other words it combines with to make natural expressions in English. Words have friends, and you need to know who they are! We call this relationship between words 'collocation'. This is a very important part of learning vocabulary.

Key words

This book practises the collocations of 270 of the most useful words in English. These 'key words' are the nouns we use to talk about particular topics. For example, nouns like *cloud, rain, snow, wind* and *fog* are key words if you want to talk about the weather.

How is the book organised?

This book is organised around topics, and divided into 22 sections. Each section consists of a number of key words. For each key word there is a box which lists its most common collocations. This is followed by exercises which help you to notice and practise the collocations of that key word in natural expressions and sentences. At the end of each section there is a test page.

How to use this book

There is simply not enough time to learn all these collocations in class, so this book is designed for self-study, and will help you to develop your vocabulary quickly and independently.

If you do one unit of this book every day, in under a year you will have learned over 2,500 expressions. That will make an enormous difference to your English!

This book can also help you with your work in class. For example, if the topic in your coursebook is about travel, then it would be a good idea to look at Section 7, Transport.

Lastly, collocation practice is one of the best ways to prepare for the PET and similar examinations, especially for the speaking and writing sections.

Keep this book!

This is a book for life. When you have completed the exercises, it becomes your personal vocabulary reference book – a resource book that you can return to again and again.

George Woolard

Edinburgh 2005

Contents

Before you begin

1. What are key words?

'Key words' are the most common and most useful words in English. They are the most important words to learn. The main reason they are important is because they can combine with lots of other words in short expressions. We call these expressions 'collocations'.

2. What are collocations?

Collocation is 'the grammar of words' – how words go together with other words. Collocation tells us which words can come before or after other words. Here are some examples from this book:

* verbs with sun

The sun rises, comes up, comes out, shines, sets, then goes down.

* adjectives with road

Roads can be clear or busy; they can be wide or narrow; they can be icy; they can be main roads.

* verbs with bottle

You can shake a bottle, then open it. You can pass a bottle to someone. You can recycle bottles.

* prepositions with phone

If you are making a phone call, you are on the phone. If you have an argument on the phone, you might put the phone down on someone – stop the call suddenly.

These are just a few of the collocations you will learn in this book.

3. Why are all the key words in this book nouns?

Nouns are the most important words we know. All the other parts of speech – adjectives, pronouns, adverbs, verbs, and prepositions – are important too, but they don't tell us as much as nouns do. Nouns tell us WHAT we are talking about:

a language

Verbs then tell us what we can do with a language:

learn it, acquire it, speak it or translate it.

Adjectives can then tell us what kind of language:

our first language, a foreign language, body language, bad language.

But the most important point is to start with ideas or things which we express with nouns.

If you are having a meal and you would like the salt, you could simply say:

salt

Everybody knows that you want the salt. So you could have said:

the salt

or   the salt, please

or   pass the salt, please

or   Could you pass the salt, please?

We know that the last sentence is the best way of saying what we want. If we had said:

Could you pass the X, please?

nobody would know what we wanted! In this situation, the noun 'salt' carries 99% of our meaning.

Key Words for Fluency – Pre-intermediate

4. Why is it important to learn the collocations of the most important nouns?

If we know 100 of the most important nouns, and we learn 10 verbs or adjectives which can go with them, we will then know 1,000 expressions. Every time we learn 100 nouns with 10 collocations of each, we add another 1,000 expressions to our vocabulary. Quite simply, learning to use more words along with the words we already know is the most useful way to expand our English. If you study all three books in this Key Words for Fluency series, you will learn over 10,000 expressions.

5. Who chose the words in this book?

These words chose themselves! In all the modern databases of English, the key words in this book are among the most commonly used. The best way for you to improve your English is to learn the most common collocations of these most common words. This pre-intermediate book contains around 10 collocations of around 270 of the most useful words at this level. That means you will practise over 2,500 useful expressions if you study this book. Dictionaries contain thousands of words and expressions, but they cannot tell you which ones to learn or how to use them. The 2,500 expressions in this book will help you to improve and become intermediate.

6. Why is this book called Key Words for Fluency?

Fluency is the ability to speak naturally, listen efficiently, read quickly, and write well. What does this mean?

1. Speaking naturally means NOT making everything up one word at a time, but speaking in whole expressions at normal speed.
2. Listening efficiently means understanding people at the speed at which they speak. This means that when you hear the first word of an expression or the first few words of a sentence, you know how it is going to end.
3. Reading quickly means that your eye is ahead of your brain! You are able to predict what the author has written.
4. Good writing is writing which expresses exactly what you want to say in natural ways which the reader will immediately understand.

All those skills depend on having a large store of words and expressions which you don't need to think about or construct every time you use English. The more collocations you know, the less you need to think! And the more fluent your English becomes.

7. Test yourself!

Here are eight common situations from this book. You should be able to guess the missing words immediately.

1. Do you like your tea strong or do you prefer it . . . . ?
    The answer is 'weak'. A person can be strong or weak. Did you know that tea or coffee can also be strong or weak?

2. I prefer my eggs scrambled. I don't really like . . . . eggs.
    The answer could be 'fried' or 'boiled' or 'poached'.

3. If you hurt your wrist badly, but it isn't broken, you . . . . it.
    'Sprain' is usually used with 'wrist' or 'ankle'. You can't 'sprain your leg' or 'sprain your arm'. This is the kind of thing you just have to learn.

4. If you have a cold, you usually have to . . . . your nose quite a lot!
    The answer is 'blow'.

5. If you want to keep your wallet safe when you're outside, don't keep it in your back pocket. Keep
    it in an . . . . pocket.
    The answer is an 'inside' pocket. That way, it is more difficult to steal.

6. If you are a child and your parents are dead, you are often brought up by . . . . parents.
    The answer is 'foster' parents. Foster parents look after children. Some then 'adopt' the child as their own.

7. If you stay away from school, you play . . . . from school.
    The answer is 'truant'. You 'play truant from school'. You are then 'a truant'.

8. If you don't know someone's telephone number, you can look it up in the telephone . . . .
    The answer is 'directory'. Some people also talk about the phone book.

9. If you give someone flowers, we say you give them a . . . . of flowers.
    The answer is 'bunch'. We also say a 'bunch of keys', and a 'bunch of bananas'.

10. If you want to borrow a newspaper, you say, 'Do you have a . . . . of yesterday's newspaper?'
    The answer is 'copy'.

Finally

I hope that these 10 examples help you understand why noticing and learning collocation is so
important:

- The more collocations you know and can use, the more fluently you will be able to
  speak. It means you won't have to make up everything new all the time – you can
  just remember whole expressions.
- The more collocations you know, the easier it will be to understand people who
  speak quickly – particularly native speakers.
- The more collocations you know, the easier it will be to read because you won't
  have to read every word.
- The more collocations you know, the easier it will be to write well and accurately.
  You won't need to translate from your own language into English as much.

Section 1

Your house

house

1. Verb + house

Complete the sentences with the correct form of the above verbs:

1. My son is at university. He . . . . a house with five other students.
2. . . . . house can be very stressful for some people.
3. It looks very old. Do you know when the house was . . . . ?
4. Somebody . . . . into our house last night and stole the television.
5. We like buying really old houses and . . . . them.
6. The house I was born in is no longer standing. It was . . . . 10 years ago.

2. Common expressions

Match the halves:

1. We've lived in
2. If you're ever passing our house,
3. I locked myself out of the house and
4. If you can't find a room in a hotel,

a. I had to climb in the bedroom window.
b. you're welcome to stay at our house.
c. the same house for over thirty years.
d. why don't you drop in for a cup of tea?

Note   We talk about *detached*, *semi-detached* and *terraced houses*.

terraced houses   semi-detached houses   a detached house

stairs

1. Verb + stairs

Complete the sentences with the correct form of the above verbs:

1. Shall we . . . . the stairs or take the lift?
2. I wish the children would stop . . . . up and down the stairs.
3. Unfortunately, I . . . . down the stairs and broke my arm.
4. My grandmother finds it difficult to . . . . the stairs these days. She's 80.

2. Common expressions

Match the halves:

1. The lift was broken, so we had to walk up	a. at the bottom of the stairs.
2. I was out of breath when I reached	b. up the stairs.
3. She picked up the child and carried him	c. the top of the stairs.
4. My bags were heavy, so I left them	d. four flights of stairs.

room

Verb + room	a tidy / an untidy room
share a room	a single / twin / double room
tidy your room	the spare room
let out rooms	the next room
Common expressions	the room is crowded
	the room is locked
a bright room	a waiting room (at the station or hospital)
a comfortable room	

1. Verb + room

Complete the sentences with the correct form of the above verbs:

1. Brian promised that he would . . . . his room, but he left it in a mess as usual.
2. I used to . . . . a room with my sister when I was young.
3. My aunt has a very large house. She . . . . out one of the rooms to a student.

2. Common expressions

Match the halves:

1. If Anne decides to stay the night,	a. The room's locked.
2. My sister's room is always tidy,	b. in the next room.
3. I'd like to book a double room	c. she can sleep in the spare room.
4. At the party the sitting room was so crowded,	d. but mine is always in a mess.
5. We'll need to find someone with a key.	e. there was nowhere to sit.
6. The kitchen is a very bright room.	f. It gets the sun most of the day.
7. I could clearly hear the television	g. were hard and very uncomfortable.
8. The seats in the waiting room	h. with a balcony and a sea view, please.

Notes

1. Note these different types of room:
   the bedroom
   the living room / the sitting room
   the dining room
   the bathroom
2. Note these expressions:
   Their living room has a wonderful view. It looks onto the lake and you can see the mountains in the distance.
   Our living room overlooks the park.
   Have you seen the film or read the book, A Room with a View?
3. Note the prepositions in these expressions:
   I looked around the room, but I couldn't see her.
   She was standing across the room from me. (on the other side of the room)

floor

Verb + floor	Common expressions
mop the floor	lie on the floor
sweep the floor	sleep on the floor
scrub the floor	slip on the (wet) floor
cover the floor (with carpets)	pile (books) on the floor
	spill (coffee) on the floor

1. Verb + floor

Complete the sentences with the correct form of the above verbs:

1. She picked up a brush and . . . . the floor.
2. Keep out of the kitchen for fifteen minutes. I've just finished . . . . the floor.
3. We . . . . the floor with newspapers before we started painting the ceiling.
4. I got down on my hands and knees and . . . . the floor clean.

2. Common expressions

Match the halves:

1. The bank robbers ordered everybody
2. Do you have a cloth?
3. We took the books down from the shelf and
4. There weren't enough beds, so some people
5. Be careful you don't slip on the wet floor.

a. I've just spilt some tea on the floor.
b. piled them on the floor.
c. I've just mopped it.
d. to lie on the floor.
e. had to sleep on the floor.

Notes

1. In the UK, we talk about the *ground / first / second floor* of a building:
   The canteen is on the ground floor of the building.
   I hope you like climbing stairs. My office is on the top floor.
2. If you drop something, it *falls on the floor*:
   Excuse me, your wallet has fallen on the floor.
3. If you drop something outside, it falls *on the ground*.

carpet

Verb + carpet			
hoover the carpet	lay a carpet	ruin a carpet	a carpet wears

Verb + carpet

Complete the sentences with the correct form of the above verbs:

1. They're coming this morning to . . . . the new carpet in the living room.
2. I . . . . the carpet in the living room when I dropped a tin of paint on it.
3. The bedroom carpet is starting to . . . . in places. We'll need to replace it soon.
4. Colin, if I clear up all the rubbish, would you . . . . the carpets?

Notes

1. Notice this expression:
   I swept the dirt under the carpet when my mother wasn't looking.
2. You clean a carpet with a *vacuum cleaner*, sometimes called *a hoover*:
   How do you expect me to hoover the carpets with this ancient hoover? It must be 30 years old!

Key Words for Fluency – Pre-intermediate

wall

Common expressions

paint a wall
a thick / thin wall
an outside wall
drill a hole in a wall
(the garden) is surrounded by a wall

cover a wall with (pictures)
a high / low wall
hang a (painting) on the wall
push (a chair) against the wall

Common expressions

Match the halves:

1. I've decided to paint
2. The house is surrounded by
3. Before you start, you'll need to drill
4. We can hear our neighbour's television
5. I pushed the bookcase back
6. The outside walls of traditional Greek houses
7. Posters of football stars
8. We hung some pictures of wild animals

a. a very high brick wall.
b. through the thin walls of our flat.
c. on the living room walls.
d. are usually painted white.
e. some holes in the wall.
f. against the living room wall.
g. the walls of my bedroom pink.
h. covered the walls of our son's bedroom.

Note   You can also stick something *on a wall* or pin something *to a wall*:
He stuck a picture of his cat on the wall above his bed.
There were some photographs from their holiday pinned to the wall.

ceiling

Common expressions

touch the ceiling
a (light) hangs from the ceiling

stare at the ceiling
a high / low ceiling

Common expressions

Complete the sentences with the correct form of the above adjectives and verbs:

1. The ceiling was so low I could . . . . it without standing on a chair.
2. The hotel rooms were pleasantly cool with large windows and . . . . ceilings.
3. I didn't get up. I just lay on my bed and . . . . at the ceiling.
4. It was a bare room with only a single light bulb . . . . from the ceiling.

Note   Note these expressions:
Water was dripping from the ceiling.
There was a large spider on the ceiling above my bed.

"I could touch the ceiling!"

door

Verb + door	Common expressions
open the door	hold the door open
close / shut the door	the door leads to the (kitchen)
slam the door	enter by the (front) door
lock the door	stand outside a door
knock on the door	There's someone at the door.
break down the door	

1. Verb + door

Complete the sentences with the correct form of the above verbs:

1. .... the door quietly behind you when you leave. Try not to .... it.
2. I always .... on my son's bedroom door before going into his room.
3. The firemen had to .... down the front door of the flat to get in.
4. Remember to .... the front door before you go to bed.

2. Common expressions:

Match the halves:

1. The burglars entered by
2. There's someone at the door.
3. This door leads to the dining room,
4. He was standing outside the door
5. Can you hold the door open for me

a. and the other one opens onto the balcony.
b. while I bring this chair in?
c. Could you see who it is?
d. the back door.
e. of the bank, waiting for it to open.

Note Note these expressions with 'door handle':
I turned the door handle and pushed the door open.
My jacket caught on the door handle as I was leaving the room.

light

Common expressions	
a light bulb	a light switch
switch the light on / off	switch off the light
leave the light on	the light is on / off
the light comes on	the light goes out

Common expressions

Match the halves:

1. I switched on the light by my bed
2. Don't forget to switch the lights off
3. The street lights come on
4. You left the light on in the bathroom
5. He must be in.
6. It was so dark that I couldn't find
7. I had to stand on a chair to change

a. at about 7 o'clock at this time of year.
b. The light in his room is still on.
c. the light bulb.
d. when you go out.
e. and read for about an hour.
f. all night again!
g. the light switch.

window

Verb + window	Common expressions
open / close a window	look through a window
break a window	the view from the window
clean the windows	the sun shines through the window
the windows steam up	see (your) reflection in the window

1. Verb + window

Complete the sentences with the correct form of the above verbs:

1. I was locked out of the house, so I had to .... a window to get in.
2. I hate .... the windows. I always pay somebody to do them for me.
3. It's quite hot in here. Do you mind if I .... a window?
4. The windows in the kitchen always .... up when I'm cooking.
   It's impossible to see through them.

2. Common expressions:

Match the halves:

1. We have a lovely view of the mountains
2. As I was passing the shop I saw
3. The early morning sun was shining through
4. I looked through all the windows of the house,

a. the kitchen window.
b. but there was nobody at home.
c. from our bedroom window.
d. my reflection in the window. I looked old!

"There's a lovely view from the window."

heating

Verb + heating	
turn the heating on / off	set the heating to come on at 5 and go off at 9
install central heating	a (house) has heating
the heating can break down	repair the central heating

Verb + heating

Complete the sentences with the correct form of the above verbs:

1. We're getting central heating .... next week. We're having two radiators in the living room, and one in each of the other rooms.
2. The heating .... down two days ago. We're still waiting for an engineer to come and .... it.
3. What kind of heating does your flat ....? Mine only has electric fires.
4. It won't take long for the room to warm up once we .... the heating on.
5. The heating is set to .... on at 6am and go off around 12 noon.
6. We usually .... off our heating during the summer months.

Test 1

house	stairs	room	floor	carpet	wall	ceiling	door	light	window	heating

1. Identifying the key word

Choose the key word which collocates with these verbs and adjectives:

1. .... let out, share, tidy, crowded, bright
2. .... break, clean, look through, open
3. .... knock on, open, lock, slam
4. .... cover, mop, scrub, slip on, sweep
5. .... lay, ruin, vacuum, wear
6. .... cover, drill into, paint, high, thick
7. .... hang from, stare at, touch, low
8. .... break into, build, demolish, live in, move
9. .... break down, install, turn on, central
10. .... climb, fall down, run up, take, use

2. The correct collocation

Choose the correct collocation in the following:

1. The house was *made / built* twenty years ago.
2. When I was a student I *hired / rented* a room in a flat.
3. Sorry, I forgot to *sweep / tidy* the floor.
4. He's old and finds it difficult to *walk / climb* the stairs.
5. Don't *slam / crash* the door when you come in.
6. The kitchen window was steamed up and I couldn't *see / watch* through it.
7. Make sure you *shut off / switch off* all the lights when you go to bed.
8. Could you *vacuum / mop* the carpets before you go out?
9. Andrew can sleep in the *added / spare* room if he's staying overnight.
10. My room is on the *high / top* floor.
11. The house has big rooms with *high / tall* ceilings.
12. I can hear my neighbour's telephone through the *slim / thin* walls of my flat.

3. Key word quiz

Complete each sentence with the correct key word:

1. I've booked a single .... at the Holiday Inn.
2. He spilt paint on the .... while he was painting the wall.
3. Remember to lock the front .... when you leave for work.
4. Someone's left the .... on in the bathroom again!
5. If you're ever passing our ...., drop in for a chat.
6. Shall we take the lift or use the ....?
7. Don't play football near the houses. You might break a ....
8. I'm afraid the .... has broken down, so it's a bit cold in here.

4. Prepositions

Choose the correct preposition to complete these expressions:

1. I dropped my pencil and it rolled *across / down* the floor.
2. I stuck a map of Malaysia *into / on* my wall.
3. We had a great view of the sea *from / in* our window.
4. There's somebody *at / in* the door. Can you see who it is?

Key Words for Fluency – Pre-intermediate

Section 2

Rooms and furniture

table

Verb + table (at home)	Verb + table (in a restaurant)	Common expressions
sit at a table	book a table	reach across the table
leave the table	manage to get a table	sit round the table
lay / set the table	be shown to your table	set a place at the table
clear the table		a coffee table

1. Verb + table

Complete the sentences with the correct form of the above verbs:

1. Roberta, would you . . . . the table while I cook breakfast? The knives and forks are in the drawer next to the fridge.
2. My father always . . . . at the top of the table when we're eating.
3. Yuan, could you . . . . the table and put the dirty dishes in the sink. I'll wash them later.
4. When I was a child, we had to ask permission before we could . . . . the dinner table.
5. We were lucky to . . . . a table. The restaurant was really busy when we got there.
6. When we arrived at the restaurant, we were . . . . to our table by the head waiter.
7. Hello. Is that the Golden Lotus? I'd like to . . . . a table for four, please. Around 8.30?

2. Common expressions

Complete the sentences with the correct preposition:

1. I've set a place for you . . . . the table. You're sitting next to Michael.
2. We'll easily get eight people . . . . the dining table for Christmas dinner.
3. I accidentally knocked over a glass of wine while I was reaching . . . . the table to get the salt.

Notes
1. Here are different kinds of table:
   kitchen table   dinner table   side table   coffee table   dining table   folding table
2. You play pool on a *pool table*, and billiards on a *billiard table*.

drawer

Common expressions	
open a drawer	look in a drawer
lock a drawer	the top / bottom drawer
at the back of the drawer	the drawer is stiff

Common expressions

Complete the sentences with the correct form of a word from the above expressions:

1. I've . . . . in all the drawers in the house, but I can't find my passport anywhere.
2. We keep the scissors in the . . . . drawer where our son can't reach them.
3. I'm having trouble opening this drawer – it's very . . . . Can you try?
4. My mother finally found her wedding ring at the . . . . of a drawer in her bedroom.
5. He . . . . the drawer of his desk and took out some writing paper.
6. I'd love to read my sister's diary, but she keeps it in a drawer in her room, which she always . . . . when she goes out.

chair

Common expressions

sit in a chair	get up from your chair
lean back in your chair	fall off your chair
push back your chair	flop into a chair

Common expressions

Complete the verb phrases with the correct preposition:

1. I put my feet up on the desk, leaned . . . . in my chair and tried to relax.
2. I don't know what's wrong with him! He just got up . . . . his chair and left without saying a word!
3. It was no accident. He fell . . . . his chair because he was drunk!
4. At the end of the meal he pushed . . . . his chair and got up to make a speech.
5. When I arrived my grandfather was sitting . . . . his favourite chair by the fire.
6. I was so tired after work, I just dropped my bags and flopped . . . . the nearest chair.

"I just flopped into a chair!"

"I just leaned back and put my feet up!"

mirror

Verb + mirror

look in the mirror
stand in front of the mirror
break a mirror

Adjective + mirror

a full-length mirror
a large / small mirror
the bathroom mirror
the hall mirror

Verb / adjective + mirror

Match the halves:

1. There's a full-length mirror behind
2. They say you get 7 years' bad luck
3. There's a large mirror,
4. She never leaves the house without
5. I find it difficult to shave
6. When I looked in the mirror,
7. Rob was standing in front of a mirror,

a. when the bathroom mirror is all steamed up.
b. trying on a new suit, when I last saw him.
c. looking at herself in the hall mirror.
d. if you break a mirror.
e. I noticed a small spot on the tip of my nose.
f. the door of the wardrobe in the bedroom.
g. hanging above the fireplace in the living room.

Note   Note these types of car mirror:
I adjusted the side mirrors, then glanced in the rear-view mirror to see if anyone was behind me.

bed

Verb + bed	Kinds of bed	Common expressions
go to bed	a single / double bed	lie in bed (all morning)
get out of bed	bunk beds	be in bed by (12) o'clock
make your bed	a soft / hard bed	spend (a week) in bed
change the bed	a spare bed	have breakfast in bed
put (the children) to bed	an unmade bed	smoke in bed
	a(n) (un)comfortable bed	be tucked up in bed

"Why do I always have to make the bed!"

"They're safely tucked up in bed!"

1. Verb + bed

Complete the sentences with the correct form of the above verbs:

1. We've trained our kids to tidy their rooms and . . . . their beds before they go to school in the morning.
2. I was very tired when I got home, so I . . . . straight to bed.
3. I had a lazy day yesterday. I didn't . . . . out of bed until lunchtime.
4. Oh, it's you, Mary! Jane's upstairs . . . . the children to bed. I'll get her to ring you back later. Is that OK?
5. I think we'd better . . . . the beds before your parents come for the weekend. You know what your mother is like!

2. Kinds of bed

Complete the sentences with one word:

1. I'm afraid we don't have a double room, but we have a twin with two . . . . beds.
2. The bed's too . . . . for me. I prefer a very hard mattress.
3. Thanks. I slept very well. It was a really . . . . bed.
4. You can spend the night here if you want – we have a . . . . bed.
5. When I was a boy, my brother and I had . . . . beds. I slept on the top . . . .
6. Our daughter's room is in a mess as usual. The bed's . . . . and there are dirty clothes all over the floor.

3. Common expressions

Match the halves:

1. Last Saturday I
2. I like to be in bed
3. My father always has
4. It can be dangerous to
5. I spent four days in bed
6. The children are safely

a. breakfast in bed on a Sunday morning.
b. with flu last week.
c. lay in bed all morning and read a book.
d. tucked up in bed.
e. smoke in bed.
f. by 10 o'clock on weekdays.

Key Words for Fluency – Pre-intermediate

sheet, blanket, pillow, mattress, wardrobe, alarm, curtains

Expressions with sheet
change the sheets
clean / dirty sheets

Expressions with blanket
an extra blanket
a warm blanket

Expressions with pillow
prop (yourself) up with a pillow
cry into your pillow

Expressions with mattress
sleep on a firm mattress
It's a very hard / soft mattress.

Expressions with wardrobe
open / close the wardrobe
hang (your shirts) in the wardrobe
a fitted wardrobe

Expressions with alarm
set the alarm (for 7 o'clock)
the alarm goes off / rings
hear the alarm

Expressions with curtains
open / close the curtains
draw the curtains

1. Verb and adjective collocations

Complete the sentences with the correct form of the above verbs or adjectives:

1. I . . . . the wardrobe, chose a shirt, then tried to decide what tie to wear with it.
2. It was colder than usual, so I put an . . . . blanket on my bed.
3. My mother always . . . . the sheets on our beds on a Sunday because Monday is her washing day.
4. I . . . . the alarm for seven, but it didn't . . . . That's why I was late for work.
5. Jack and Sue want to stay over on Saturday night. Could you put some . . . . sheets on the bed in the spare room?
6. The first thing I do when I get out of bed in the morning is to . . . . the curtains, and see what the weather's like.
7. All the bedrooms in our new flat have . . . . wardrobes, so there's plenty of storage space for our clothes.

"I'll just draw the curtains."

2. Preposition focus

Complete the sentences with the correct preposition:

1. Can you hang these trousers . . . . the wardrobe please?
2. I prefer to sleep . . . . a firm mattress. If it's too soft, I find it gives me a sore back.
3. I propped myself up . . . . a couple of pillows, so that I could read comfortably in bed.
4. When I went into her room, Farah was crying . . . . her pillow. She was obviously still upset about splitting up from her boyfriend.

Notes

1. Note these expressions:
   I was so tired last night. I was asleep before my head hit the pillow!
   When my parents turn the lights out, I read my book under the blankets with a torch.
2. Note that we usually refer to an alarm clock as 'an alarm'.
   Don't forget to set the alarm. We have to be up early tomorrow.
3. *Draw the curtains* can mean either *open* or *close* them.

bath and shower

Verb + bath / shower	**Verb + bath**
have / take a bath / shower	lie in the bath
get into the bath / shower	run a bath
get out of the bath /shower	the bath overflows
clean the bath / shower	**Verb + shower**
Adjective + bath /shower	turn on / off the shower
a hot bath / shower	have a quick shower
a long bath / shower	have a cold shower

"The bath has overflowed!"

"There's nothing I like better than a long bath."

1. Verb + bath / shower

Complete the sentences with the correct form of the above verbs:

1. I undressed quickly and . . . . into the bath.
2. How often do you . . . . a bath?
3. When I . . . . out of the shower, I discovered there were no towels in the bathroom!
4. Don't forget to . . . . the bath when you've finished. There's a cloth under the basin.

Complete the sentences with either bath or shower:

5. I'll be home in about twenty minutes. Could you run a . . . . for me, please?
6. I turned off the . . . . and reached for a towel.
7. My brother lies in the . . . . for ages, which means that nobody else can get into the bathroom!
8. Marta! Run up to the bathroom and turn the water off before the . . . . overflows.

2. Adjective collocations

Complete the sentences with the above adjectives:

1. Have I got time for a . . . . shower before we have to leave for the theatre?
2. I had a . . . ., hot bath after the game to soothe my aching muscles. I soaked for nearly an hour.
3. He has a . . . . shower every morning to waken himself up. I don't know how he can do that!
4. I love standing under a . . . . shower when I get back from work in the evening. It only takes a couple of minutes to relax the tense muscles in my neck.

Note Note these common expressions:
Could you see who is at the door? I'm in the bath.
Turn the taps off or the bath will overflow!

towel

Common expressions	
a clean / dirty towel	a dry / wet towel
a dish towel	a beach towel
a bath towel	paper towels
dry yourself with a towel	

Common expressions

Match the halves:

1. There are no paper towels in the washroom
2. If there's one thing I hate,
3. I dried myself with your towel by mistake.
4. There's nothing nicer
5. I can't find a clean dish towel anywhere,
6. Sorry, I've spilt some coffee on the carpet.
7. We can buy beach towels when we get there.

a. so I'm afraid I can't dry the dishes!
b. They're much cheaper in Spain.
c. Have you a cloth or some paper towels?
d. it's dirty towels!
e. It's exactly the same as mine!
f. and the electric hand drier is broken!
g. than a lovely soft clean bath towel!

Note   Note that we talk about a *bath towel*, but a *face cloth*.

toilet

Verb + toilet	Toilet + noun	Adjective + toilet
need the toilet	toilet facilities	ladies / gents toilets
go to the toilet	toilet paper	public toilets
use the toilet	the toilet seat	disabled toilet
flush the toilet		
Have you been to the ... ?		

1. Verb and adjective collocations

Complete the sentences with the correct form of the above verbs and adjectives:

1. Don't forget to wash your hands after you've . . . . to the toilet.
2. I . . . . the toilet, so can you stop the video for a few minutes?
3. We couldn't use the . . . . toilets in the park because they had been vandalised.
4. Nobody could . . . . the toilet because it was out of order.
5. Excuse me, is there a . . . . toilet? My friend is in a wheelchair.
6. There was a sign above the toilet bowl which said, 'Please . . . . toilet when finished'.
7. There was a queue outside the . . . . toilets. Why is there never one outside the gents?

2. Toilet + noun

Complete the sentences with the above nouns:

1. Maria, we're out of toilet . . . . Could you get some when you're out?
2. I wish your grandfather would remember to put the toilet . . . . up!
3. There was no wheelchair access and no disabled toilet . . . . at the concert.

Notes   1. The informal word 'loo' is often used for toilet:
I'll just go to the loo before the film starts.
2. In the UK public toilets are sometimes called *public conveniences*.
3. In the US, the toilet in your home is the *bathroom,* and in a public place it is the *rest room.*

Test 2

table	drawer	chair	mirror	bed	sheet	blanket	pillow
mattress	wardrobe	alarm	curtains	bath	shower	towel	toilet

1. Identifying the key word

Choose the key word which collocates with these verbs and adjectives:

1. . . . .   fall off, get up from, push back, sit in
2. . . . .   change, go to, lie in, make, hard
3. . . . .   go off, hear, set
4. . . . .   clear, leave, reach across, set, sit at
5. . . . .   break, look in, full-length, large
6. . . . .   flush, go to, need, use, public
7. . . . .   lock, look in, open, stiff, top
8. . . . .   dry yourself with, dirty, wet
9. . . . .   run, clean, have, get into, lie in
10. . . . .   quick, cold, get into, have, turn on

2. The correct collocation

Choose the correct collocation:

1. Andrew, could you *make / lay* the table for dinner, please?
2. I can't open this drawer. It's really *hard / stiff.*
3. When I finished the letter, I *fell / leaned* back in my chair and looked out of the window.
4. I never *look / see* in the mirror first thing in the morning!
5. Make sure you *change / clean* your bed at least once a week.
6. I set the alarm for 7am, but for some reason it didn't *go / come* off.
7. Could you *make / run* the bath for me?
8. Have I got time for a *quick / short* shower before we go out?

3. Key word quiz

Complete each sentence with the correct key word:

1. Excuse me, but this . . . . is wet. Have you got a dry one?
2. Harry's room's in a mess again. He hasn't even made his . . . . yet.
3. My grandfather is now 90 and needs help to get in and out of the . . . .
4. We all sat around the kitchen . . . . , drinking tea and chatting.
5. It's going to be a cold night. Can I have an extra . . . . on my bed?
6. I put my passport in the . . . . by my bed, and locked it before going out.
7. Could you hang these shirts up in the . . . . , please?
8. I always close the . . . . when I go to bed. I never sleep with them open!
9. Unfortunately, there were no . . . . facilities at the bus station.
10. Make sure you turn off the . . . . when you've finished.

4. Prepositions

Choose the correct preposition to complete these expressions:

1. I was so tired I couldn't get *out / up* from my chair.
2. I reached *across / along* the table to get the salt.
3. I prefer to sleep *in / on* a firm mattress.
4. I'm usually *in / into* bed by ten o'clock most days.
5. My brother lies *in / on* the bath for hours after playing football.

Section 3

In the kitchen

kettle, cooker, oven, freezer, dishwasher, washing machine, grill, fridge, toaster

kettle

switch on the kettle

switch off the kettle

fill the kettle

boil the kettle

cooker

turn the cooker on / off

leave the cooker on

put (a pot) on the cooker

oven

put (the chicken) in the oven

remove (the cake) from the oven

turn the oven to (200°)C

freezer

take (the meat) out of the freezer

put (the fish) in the freezer

dishwasher

load the dishwasher

empty the dishwasher

washing machine

put (clothes) in the washing machine

empty the washing machine

fridge

put (milk) in the fridge

keep (medicines) in the fridge

chill (wine) in the fridge

(fish) keeps in the fridge (for 24 hours)

grill

cook something under the grill

toaster

put a slice of bread in the toaster

1. Verb collocations

Complete the sentences with the correct form of the above verbs:

1. Hang on a minute. I think I've . . . . the cooker on. I'll just go and . . . . it off.
2. . . . . the oven on low, and cook the casserole very slowly.
3. Could you . . . . the kettle on and make some tea?
4. You'll have to . . . . the dishwasher before you can put the dirty plates in.
5. Don't leave your dirty clothes on the floor! . . . . them in the washing machine!
6. That reminds me. I must . . . . the chicken out of the freezer and defrost it for tonight's dinner.
7. Could you . . . . two slices of bread in the toaster for me, please?

2. Preposition focus

Complete the sentences with the correct preposition:

1. Rub the chicken with garlic before putting it . . . . the oven.
2. Cook the fish . . . . a hot grill for 5 minutes.
3. Is it OK if I put my dirty jeans . . . . the washing machine?
4. Remove the cakes . . . . the oven, and allow them to cool before eating them.

3. Common expressions

Match the halves:

1. The milk will go off quite quickly	a. keep it in the fridge.
2. Don't forget to chill	b. if you don't put it in the fridge.
3. Spoon the extra sauce into a jar and	c. a couple of days in the fridge.
4. The meat should keep for	d. the wine in the fridge.

knife, fork and spoon

knife / fork / spoon
hold your knife / fork / spoon
pick up / put down your . . .

spoon
a soup spoon
a teaspoon
a serving spoon
a wooden spoon
stir (the soup) with a spoon

knife
a sharp / blunt knife
cut / slice (meat) with a knife

fork
pick (food) up with your fork
beat (eggs) with a fork

peeling a potato   picking up peas   beating eggs with a fork   slicing bread

serving yourself   using a knife and fork   stirring the soup

1. Verb collocations

Complete the sentences with the correct form of the above verbs:

1. Peter! . . . . your knife and fork down, and wait until everybody has been served.
2. I . . . . up my spoon and tried the soup, but I wasn't hungry.
3. My brother is right-handed, but he . . . . his fork in his right hand, and his knife in his left!

2. Adjective and noun collocations

Complete the sentences with the above adjectives and nouns:

1. I can't peel the potatoes with this knife. It's far too . . . .
2. Jane! Use the . . . . spoon to lift the vegetables onto your plate, not your fingers!
3. You'll need a . . . . knife to cut your steak. It's very tough.
4. Have you got a . . . . ? I take sugar in my coffee.

3. Common expressions

Match the halves:

1. Stir the soup occasionally
2. Can you cut the melon in half
3. I tried to pick the peas up with my fork
4. Beat the eggs and flour with a fork

a. but they kept falling off.
b. until the mixture is smooth.
c. with the kitchen knife, please?
d. with the wooden spoon.

Note   Note these expressions:
Be careful you don't cut yourself with that knife!
I can't believe that some ten-year-old kids don't know how to use a knife and fork!

cupboard

Verb + cupboard	Adjective + cupboard
keep (glasses) in a cupboard	an empty cupboard
fill a cupboard with (food)	a locked cupboard
put (cups) away in a cupboard	
clean out a cupboard	

Verb / adjective + cupboard

Complete the sentences with the correct form of the above verbs and adjectives:

1. We . . . . all our medicines in a . . . . cupboard, well out of the reach of our kids.
2. I found the missing key while I was . . . . out the cupboards.
3. We . . . . the cupboard with lots of food – more than enough to last the entire holiday.
4. I folded the dish towels and . . . . them away in the cupboard.
5. The cupboards were . . . . and there was nothing to eat in the whole house.

"The cupboard is well out of reach of the kids."   "The cupboard is empty."   "I can't reach the shelf."   "The shelf just collapsed!"

shelf

Verb + shelf	Adjective + shelf
put up shelves	the top / bottom / middle shelf
put (the pots) on a shelf	
get (a plate) down from a shelf	
shelves collapse	

Verb and adjective collocations

Complete the sentences with the correct form of the above verbs and adjectives:

1. The shelf . . . . under the weight of the plates. There were far too many on it!
2. I had to get my brother to . . . . up some shelves in my kitchen. I'm useless at DIY!
3. Just . . . . the cookery book back on the shelf above the fridge when you've finished.
4. I can't reach the sugar on the . . . . shelf. Could you . . . . it down for me, please?

Notes
1. Food is placed on shelves in shops and supermarkets:
   I got a job filling shelves at the local supermarket.
2. 'Shelf life' is the length of time a product such as food remains fresh for sale:
   Strawberries have a very short shelf life. (They go bad quickly.)

pot and pan

<table>
<tr><td>Verb + pot / pan</td><td>Types of pots and pans</td></tr>
<tr><td>fill a pot (with water)</td><td>a frying pan</td></tr>
<tr><td>cover a pot (with a lid)</td><td>a chip pan</td></tr>
<tr><td>clean a pot</td><td>a saucepan</td></tr>
<tr><td>cook (the potatoes) in a pot</td><td>a soup pot</td></tr>
<tr><td>Common expressions</td><td>a cooking pot</td></tr>
<tr><td>a set of pots and pans</td><td>a coffee pot</td></tr>
<tr><td>the bottom of the pot</td><td>a teapot</td></tr>
<tr><td>heat (the soup) in a pot</td><td>a flower pot</td></tr>
<tr><td>put a pot on (the cooker)</td><td></td></tr>
<tr><td>remove a pot from (the cooker)</td><td></td></tr>
</table>

a teapot   a coffee pot   a saucepan   a soup pot   a cooking pot   a frying pan   a flower pot

1. Verb + pot / pan

Complete the sentences with the correct form of the above verbs:

1. . . . . the pot with water, then bring it to the boil before adding the pasta.
2. . . . . the pan with a lid, and let the stew cook slowly until the meat is tender.
3. I hate . . . . greasy pots and pans.
4. . . . . the peas in that small pot over there.

2. Common expressions

Match the halves:

1. I'm thinking of buying my mother	a. the bottom of the pot.
2. I put the pot of soup	b. and leave it to cool.
3. The heat was too high and I burnt	c. a new set of pots and pans for her birthday.
4. Remove the pot from the heat,	d. then add the meat and onions.
5. Heat the oil in a large frying pan,	e. on the cooker to heat it up.

3. Kinds of pots and pans

Complete the following expressions:

1. make tea in a . . . .
2. fry chips in a . . . .
3. make a stew in a . . . .
4. fry eggs in a . . . .
5. serve the soup straight from the . . . .
6. put the plant in a . . . .
7. serve the coffee in a . . . .
8. buy a new set of . . . .

Notes

1. Note these ways of describing food which is cooking in a pot or pan:
   A pot of soup was simmering on the cooker; the sausages were sizzling in the frying pan.
2. Note this expression:
   I left the dirty pots and pans in the sink to soak.
3. A *pot plant* is one which you grow indoors in a pot – not outside in the garden.

plate

Common expressions	Types of plate
a waiter clears your plate away	an empty plate
drop a plate	a dinner plate
smash a plate	a soup plate
pile plates (in the sink)	a dirty / clean plate
heap food on your plate	
a plate of salad	

1. Common expressions

Complete the sentences with the correct form of the above verbs:

1. I . . . . one of my mother's favourite plates on the floor and it . . . . How can I tell her? She's going to be very upset.
2. We all rushed to the buffet and . . . . food onto our plates. We were absolutely starving!
3. At the end of the meal, we . . . . the dirty plates in the sink and left them overnight.
4. When we had finished eating, the waitress . . . . away our plates, and brought coffee.

2. Types of plate

Match the halves:

1. Could you get the soup plates, please.
2. Would you take away the dinner plates and
3. Waiter! This plate's dirty.
4. He looked up from his empty plate and

   a. asked if there was any more paella.
   b. Could you bring me a clean one, please?
   c. bring some bowls for the sweet?
   d. It's ready to serve.

a bowl of soup   *a sugar bowl*   *a bowl of salad*   *a pile of plates*   *a plate of soup*   *a dinner plate*

bowl

Common expressions	
have a bowl of (rice)	fill a bowl with (cereal)
empty (a packet) into a bowl	lick your bowl clean
a sugar / fruit / salad / rice bowl	a bowl of salad / rice / soup

Common expressions

Complete the sentences with the correct form of the above verbs:

1. My daughter . . . . her bowl to the top with corn flakes, then poured milk over them.
2. I opened the soup packet and . . . . the contents into a bowl.
3. I don't eat much for breakfast. I usually only . . . . a small bowl of cereal.
4. My five-year-old loves . . . . his bowl clean at the dinner table, but he knows not to do it if we have guests!

sink

Verb + sink

Complete the sentences with the correct form of the above verbs:

1. I . . . . the sink with hot soapy water to do the washing up.
2. Just . . . . the unwashed dishes in the sink and we'll wash them in the morning.
3. The coffee tasted awful, so I . . . . it down the sink.
4. When I arrived, Tom was . . . . at the sink, washing his socks.
5. Don't . . . . the sink at the moment – it's . . . . I'm waiting for the plumber to come and fix it.

"The sink is blocked!"

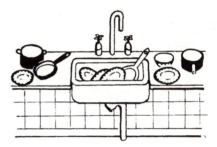

"He left a huge pile of dirty dishes in the sink!"

dishes

Common expressions

Match the halves:

1. If you clear the dishes from the table,   a. when I'm washing the dishes.
2. I always wear rubber gloves   b. dry the dishes.
3. There was a huge pile   c. on the draining board by the sink.
4. I grabbed a dish towel and helped to   d. I'll start the washing up.
5. We stacked the clean dishes   e. of unwashed dishes in the sink.

Test 3

cupboard	shelf	kettle	cooker	oven	freezer	grill	fridge
toaster	plate	bowl	knife	fork	spoon	pot	pan
dishwasher	washing machine		sink	dishes			

1. The correct collocation

Choose the correct collocation:

1. *Switch on / Switch* the kettle and I'll make some tea.
2. Like most people I *carry / hold* my fork in my left hand.
3. Have you got a wooden spoon? I need to *stir / turn* the soup in the pot.
4. We *filled / loaded* the cupboard with pasta and tinned food.
5. Could you help me to *put up / put in* some shelves in the kitchen?
6. *Close / Cover* the pot with a lid and leave it for 20 minutes.
7. The *dinner / lunch* plate was so hot I couldn't pick it up.
8. You can't use the sink. It's *blocked / broken*.
9. There's a *heap / pile* of dirty dishes in the sink and it's not my turn to wash them!

2. Key word quiz

Complete each sentence with the correct key word:

1. This . . . . is blunt. Have you got a sharp one?
2. The . . . . are empty. We'll need to do some shopping.
3. Put the chicken in the . . . . and roast it for about two hours.
4. I accidentally dropped a flower . . . . on the floor.
5. Could you clear the dirty dishes from the table and load the . . . . , please?
6. Has the . . . . boiled yet? I'm dying for a cup of coffee.
7. Could you empty the . . . . and put the clothes in the tumble dryer?
8. I put a little oil in a large frying . . . . and then added the onions.
9. The kitchen . . . . was filled with soapy water.
10. Put the leftover salad in the . . . . We can have it for lunch tomorrow.
11. I hate washing . . . . , but I don't mind drying them.
12. Put the soup pot on the . . . . on a low heat.

3. Prepositions

Choose the correct preposition to complete these expressions:

1. Could you turn the oven *at / to* 180°C.
2. I cooked the fish slowly *on / under* the grill.
3. Fill the pot with water and put it *in / on* the cooker to boil.
4. Could you clear the dirty dishes *from / out of* the table, please?
5. I must remember to take the meat *into / out of* the freezer for tonight's dinner.
6. Can you get me that pot down *from / on* the top shelf? I can't reach it.
7. Put a couple of slices of bread *in / on* the toaster for me.
8. I poured the dirty water *down / in* the sink.
9. I sliced the vegetables *by / with* a sharp knife.
10. Heat the soup up *in / on* a pot and serve immediately.

Section 4

Sky and weather

sky

Common expressions

Match the halves:

1. A huge fire at a nearby factory
2. I like to see the sun. Grey skies
3. I think the sky's beginning to clear.
4. A few white clouds drifted
5. The sky suddenly darkened when
6. We looked out at a clear blue sky.

a. I can see a few blue patches among the clouds.
b. the sun moved behind some black clouds.
c. lit up the night sky.
d. There wasn't a cloud in sight!
e. make me feel depressed.
f. across the sky.

Note   Note this expression:
The castle stood out against the evening sky.

sun

1. Verb + sun

Complete the sentences with the correct form of the above verbs:

1. After ten minutes the rain stopped, and the sun . . . . out again.
2. I love to get up early and watch the sun . . . .
3. Be careful when you're on holiday. Put on lots of sun cream and . . . . the midday sun.
4. We sat drinking beer by the sea, watching the sun . . . . down.

2. Common expressions:

Match the halves:

1. We dried our
2. I wear a baseball cap
3. I can't sit in the sun for very long.
4. I can't see a thing.

a. I've got very fair skin.
b. wet swimming costumes in the sun.
c. The sun's in my eyes.
d. to shield my eyes from the sun.

Note   Note these common expressions:
We're having a great time here, soaking up the sun.
During the holidays we lazed around in the sun all day long.
I've got sunburn on the back of my neck. I must remember to wear a hat next time.

moon

Common expressions

Complete the sentences with the correct form of the above verbs:

1. The moon . . . . behind the clouds and it was difficult to see where we were going.
2. When the moon . . . . out from behind the clouds, we were able to see the path clearly.
3. The moon was . . . . so brightly I could read my book without a torch.
4. I watched the full moon . . . . up over the horizon. It was enormous!
5. We could . . . . the lions quite easily by the light of the moon.
6. During Ramadan, Muslims do not eat or drink during the day. Ramadan lasts for about a month and ends when the new moon . . . .

star

Common expressions

Match the halves:

1. It was so hot that we slept outside,
2. It was a clear night with no moon and
3. I lay on my back and looked up
4. Capella is one of

a. at the stars.
b. the brightest stars in the sky.
c. beneath the stars.
d. the stars were shining brightly.

Notes
1. Note the expression:
   It was a clear cold night and the stars were all out. (shining)
2. If someone is *a star*, they are famous in the world of entertainment or sport.

rain

Verb + rain	Noun + preposition + rain	Adjective + rain
rain starts / stops	a drop of rain	heavy / torrential / light rain
rain spreads	a possibility of rain	**Common expressions**
the rain held off	a shower of rain	take shelter from the rain
get caught in the rain	the sound of rain	get (soaking) wet in the rain
pour with rain	a break in the rain	bring (it) in out of the rain
rain beat against (the window)		

1. Verb + rain

Complete the sentences with the correct form of the above verbs:

1. When we were in Wales, it . . . . with rain from the moment we arrived.
2. I . . . . caught in the rain and was soaked from head to toe.
3. I hope the rain . . . . off until we get home. I don't have a coat or an umbrella with me.
4. The rain . . . . against my bedroom window all night and kept me awake.
5. Heavy rain is falling in Rome this morning and will . . . . later to the north of the country.
6. I ran for shelter as soon as the rain . . . .

2. Adjective + rain

Match the halves:

1. The weather forecast says	a. the rain was very light.
2. I didn't need my umbrella as	b. through the torrential rain.
3. I had to drive very slowly	c. we're in for more heavy rain tomorrow.

3. Noun + preposition + rain

Complete the sentences with the above nouns:

1. According to the forecast, there's a strong . . . . of rain this afternoon.
2. I'm sure I felt a few . . . . of rain on my face just now.
3. There was hardly a . . . . in the rain all day. It never really stopped once!
4. Our barbecue was ruined by a heavy . . . . of rain.
5. We couldn't hear ourselves talking for the . . . . of rain on the roof of the car.

4. Common expressions

Complete these sentences with the correct preposition:

1. We took shelter . . . . the rain in a nearby café.
2. We got soaking wet . . . . the rain on the way home from school.
3. Shouldn't we bring the washing in out . . . . the rain?
4. It was a miserable day. It poured . . . . rain all afternoon.

Notes
1. Note these expressions:
   It looks like rain to me. (I think it's going to rain.)
   I hope the rain lets up for the weekend. (finally stops)
   This rain looks as if it has set in for the rest of the day. (started and will continue)
   The rain is expected to last all weekend. (will continue)
2. Notice these ways of saying the rain was very heavy:
   It was pouring with rain. or *It was pouring.*
   It was bucketing with rain. or *It was bucketing.*

thunder and lightning

Common expressions

Match the halves:

1. During the storm, lightning
2. There was a sudden flash of lightning,
3. Tom was struck by lightning
4. Can lightning ever strike

a. twice in the same place?
b. flashed across the sky.
c. followed by a loud clap of thunder.
d. while playing golf.

Notes
1. You can also say *a thunder clap* as well as *a clap of thunder*.
2. Notice from the exercise that lightning *flashes across the sky*.

"Struck by lightning!"

cloud

1. Verb + cloud

Complete the sentences with the correct form of the above verbs:

1. It was a fine day when we got there. Only a few clouds were . . . . across the sky.
2. Dark clouds suddenly . . . . the sun and I had to put a jumper on.
3. A few minutes after take-off our plane . . . . through the clouds into bright sunlight.
4. Later in the day the clouds . . . . , and the mountains suddenly came into view.

2. Adjective + cloud

Complete the sentences with the above adjectives:

1. Black . . . . clouds were gathering on the horizon, so we left the beach and went back to our hotel before the rain started.
2. It was a beautiful summer's day with just a few, fluffy . . . . clouds in the sky.
3. Visibility at the airport was poor because of the . . . . cloud and heavy rain.
4. We couldn't see the top of Mount Everest. It was covered in . . . . cloud.

Note
Note these noun + preposition + cloud expressions:
The whole country was covered in a blanket of cloud.
There were a few breaks in the cloud later in the day, so we got some sunshine.

snow

Verb + snow	Adjective + snow	Noun + of + snow
snow falls	deep snow	a blanket of snow
snow drifts	heavy snow	a fall of snow
snow melts	melting snow	a flake of snow (snowflake)
clear snow (from a path)		

1. Verb + snow

Complete the sentences with the correct form of the above verbs:

1. The snow has been . . . . steadily all day. It's now about 10 centimetres deep.
2. It took me over an hour to . . . . the snow from my front door to the street.
3. I don't think the snow will lie on the streets for very long. It's already starting to . . . .
4. Snow had . . . . against the garage door overnight and I couldn't push it open.

2. Adjective + snow

Match the halves:

1. We had to struggle through	a. by heavy snow. All main roads are closed.
2. The melting snow has caused	b. deep snow to get here. It was knee-deep in places.
3. Many villages have been cut off	c. severe flooding in the area.

3. Noun + of + snow

Complete the sentences with the above nouns:

1. The day was cold, with frequent . . . . of snow which only lasted a few minutes.
2. A few . . . . of snow fell, but it never really started to snow properly.
3. Fresh snow fell during the night. The ground was covered in a thick . . . . of snow when we got up.

ice

Verb + ice		Adjective + ice
ice forms	be covered with ice	thick ice
ice melts	skate on ice	thin ice
ice cracks	skid on ice	black ice
scrape ice off (your car)	slip on ice	

Verb + ice

Complete the sentences with the correct form of the above verbs:

1. The sun came out and . . . . the ice on the pavements.
2. Do you think the ice on the pond is now thick enough to . . . . on?
3. My friend's car . . . . on some black ice and hit a tree.
4. The lake is usually . . . . with thick ice for most of January and February.
5. My mother broke her arm when she . . . . on some ice and fell.
6. As soon as I stood on the thin ice, it started to . . . . I got off it very quickly!
7. Ice had . . . . on the windscreen of my car overnight. I had to . . . . it off before I could drive to work.

wind

Common expressions
the wind blows
the wind changes
the wind rises / gets up
the wind drops / dies down
the wind whistles (through trees)
cycle / walk / sail into the wind
shelter from / out of the wind

Adjective + wind
strong / high winds
a light wind
icy / cold / bitter winds

---

1. Common expressions

Complete the sentences with the correct form of the above verbs:

1. The wind suddenly . . . . direction and started to . . . . from the north.
2. I think we should wait till the wind . . . . before we try to put up the tent.
3. You could hear the wind . . . . through the small gaps in the windows.
4. We didn't reach the top of the mountain. We decided to turn back when the wind started to . . . .
5. I'm getting cold. Let's . . . . from the wind in that shop doorway over there.
6. The captain said that the ferry would be thirty minutes late because it was . . . . into a very strong wind.

2. Adjective + wind

Match the halves:

1. The flags on top of the castle fluttered gently
2. Last night's high winds caused
3. The wind was so strong
4. The icy wind cut right through me.

a. it almost blew me off my feet.
b. I was absolutely freezing when I got home.
c. in the light wind.
d. serious damage to our roof.

Note   Note these noun + preposition + wind expressions:
It was absolutely still. There wasn't a breath of wind.
A strong gust of wind blew my hat off my head.

fog

Common expressions
fog rolls in
be / get lost in thick fog

fog lifts / clears
heavy / thick / dense fog

Common expressions

Complete the sentences with the correct form of the above verbs:

1. The fog is beginning to . . . ., so our plane should be able to take off soon.
2. We were hopelessly . . . . in thick fog. We stopped at a petrol station to ask where we were. They must have thought we were mad!
3. It was lovely and sunny when we arrived at the beach, but when the fog . . . . in from the sea, we had to go home. It got so cold very quickly!

Test 4

1. Identifying the key word

Choose the key word which collocates with these verbs and adjectives:

1. .... appear, shine, full, new
2. .... get caught in, pour with, start, heavy
3. .... blow, change, drop, high
4. .... float, dark, low, storm
5. .... comes out, rise, set, shine
6. .... look up at, sleep under, shine, bright
7. .... fall, melt, deep, heavy
8. .... clear, roll in, thick, heavy
9. .... crack, form, melt, thin
10. .... brighten, look up at, clear, blue

2. The correct collocation

Choose the correct collocation:

1. The sky *cleared / emptied* and the sun came out.
2. It's a good idea to *avoid / miss* the hot midday sun.
3. It was easy to see where we were going because of the *complete / full* moon.
4. There was no moon and the stars were *flashing / shining* brightly.
5. I got soaking wet in the *heavy / strong* rain.
6. During the storm lightning *flashed / shone* across the sky.
7. The low cloud *lifted / went up* and we were able to see the top of the mountain.
8. There was a heavy *drop / fall* of snow overnight.
9. Ice *forms / is made* on the lake in winter.
10. It was difficult to walk in the *heavy / high* winds.

3. Key word quiz

Complete each sentence with the correct key word:

1. I needed my sunglasses to drive because the .... was in my eyes.
2. The .... is very deep in places. Over 40cm fell last night.
3. A strong .... was blowing when we arrived in Sydney.
4. We should see the new .... tonight.
5. I got caught in the .... without an umbrella as I left work.
6. The plane landed safely after it was struck by ....
7. I looked out of my window at a clear, blue ....
8. The .... on the lake is very thin, so don't walk on it.
9. You couldn't see two metres in front of you in the thick ....
10. It's a bit cloudy tonight, so you won't be able to see so many ....

4. Prepositions

Choose the correct preposition to complete these expressions:

1. We slept on the beach *below / under* the stars.
2. The moon disappeared *behind / under* a cloud.
3. We took shelter *from / out* the rain under a large tree.
4. We got lost *in / inside* thick fog on our way down the mountain.

Section 5

The natural world

sea

Common expressions	Adjective + sea
swim in the sea	heavy / rough seas
dive into the sea	a calm / flat sea
drown at sea	the open sea
live by the sea	
go by sea	

1. Prepositions

Compete the sentences with the correct preposition:

1. Living in Birmingham is OK, but I'd like to live . . . . the sea.
2. The whole family went swimming . . . . the sea.
3. I dived off the side of the boat . . . . the sea.
4. Because it is an island, most of Britain's exports go . . . . sea.
5. My grandfather drowned . . . . sea when his fishing boat sank in a storm.

2. Adjective + sea

Match the halves:

1. The sea was very calm.
2. The crew were rescued minutes before
3. The ferry left the harbour and
4. A fishing boat is missing

a. the boat sank in heavy seas.
b. It was like glass.
c. in rough seas off the Italian coast.
d. headed out towards the open sea.

Notes

1. Note these ways of describing where something is:
   The town is 2000 metres above sea level.
   The lake is almost 600 feet below sea level.
   The Titanic lies on the sea bed, 12,000 feet below the surface.
   The documentary was about creatures that live at the bottom of the sea.

2. There are different ways of saying that you work at sea:
   My father is an officer in the navy. My uncle is a seaman in the merchant navy.

wave

common expressions	
waves break on the shore	waves crash against (the boat, rocks)
waves lap against (the boat, rocks)	surf the waves
a huge wave	a tidal wave

Common expressions

Match the halves:

1. There were hundreds of young people out
2. A tidal wave struck the town,
3. The little boat capsized after it was hit
4. Huge waves were crashing
5. The waves lapped
6. We sat on the beach watching the waves

a. breaking on the shore.
b. against the rocks.
c. surfing the huge waves.
d. gently against the side of the boat.
e. by a huge wave.
f. destroying almost all the buildings.

river

"I spent the afternoon down at the river, fishing."

"This is the old bridge across the river."

"The river's being polluted by waste from the local factory."

1. Verb + river

Complete the sentences with the correct form of the above verbs:

1. Two major rivers . . . . through our town.
2. The river . . . . over completely during the freezing weather.
3. The only way to . . . . the river is by ferry. There isn't a bridge for miles.
4. Waste from factories continues to . . . . our rivers, killing fish and wildlife.

2. Adjective + river

Complete the sentences with the correct form of the above adjectives:

1. Is the Nile the . . . . river in the world or is it the Mississippi?
2. I don't think we'll be able to swim across the river at this point. It's far too . . . .
3. The river's quite deep here. Let's try to cross further up. It looks . . . . there.

3. Common expressions

Match the halves. Then underline the prepositions.

1. I caught six fish	a. across the river.
2. We were only able to sail	b. into the river.
3. They're building a new bridge	c. in the River Tyne at the weekend.
4. The boat drifted slowly	d. along the river bank.
5. After dinner we went for a walk	e. down the river towards the open sea.
6. I slipped on the wet ground and fell	f. up the river as far as the dam.

Note   One side of a river is called the *river bank*. Both sides are the *banks* of the river.
The river overflowed its banks after a week of heavy rainfall.
The village was flooded when the river rose and burst its banks.

island

Verb + island	Adjective + island
live on an island	a desert island
get to / reach an island	a remote island
visit an island	a tropical island
leave an island	an island is uninhabited
sail round an island	
islands attract (tourists)	

1. Verb + island

Complete the sentences with the correct form of the above verbs:

1. The only way to . . . . to the island is by boat. A daily ferry connects it to the mainland.
2. Are there people on the island? I thought nobody . . . . there.
3. Many of the young people are forced to . . . . the island to find work on the mainland.
4. We'll be . . . . a number of Greek islands on our Mediterranean cruise.
5. The island is a popular holiday resort. It . . . . around 80,000 tourists a year.
6. We . . . . round the island in the middle of the lake, but there was nothing much to see.

2. Adjective + island

Complete the sentences with the above adjectives:

1. It's such a . . . . island that very few tourists go there. It's so difficult to get to.
2. What would you take with you if you had to spend some time alone on a . . . . island?
3. My idea of the perfect holiday would be two weeks on a . . . . island in the Pacific Ocean!
4. The island of St Kilda is . . . . Nobody lives there any more. It's off the west coast of Scotland.

beach

Verb + beach	Adjective + beach	Common expressions
go to the beach	a beautiful beach	spend the day at the beach
lie on the beach	a sandy beach	stroll along the beach
clean up the beach	a private beach	people flock to the beach
the beach stretches for (miles)	an unspoilt beach	a beach holiday
	a dirty beach	something is washed up on the beach
	the whole beach	

1. Verb + beach

Complete the sentences with the correct form of the above verbs:

1. There's nothing I like better than a beach holiday somewhere really warm. I just love . . . . on the beach, sunbathing all day long.
2. The beach is very dirty . They need to . . . . it up.
3. Our kids love . . . . to the beach.
4. When we went to Cuba, our hotel was right on the beach. It . . . . for miles in each direction, as far as the eye could see.

2. Adjective + beach

Match the halves:

1. Tourism is new to the area	a. It's contaminated with raw sewage.
2. I had the whole beach to myself.	b. endless sandy beaches and perfect weather.
3. Be careful. The local beach is dirty.	c. so you'll find a lot of unspoilt beaches.
4. The east coast of the country is famous	d. private beach with a bar.
5. Tourists are attracted to the area by its	e. There wasn't another soul in sight!
6. The hotel has a	f. for its beautiful beaches.

3. Common expressions

Complete the sentences with the correct preposition:

1. We strolled barefoot . . . . the beach.
2. Because of the good weather, thousands of tourists are flocking . . . . the beaches today.
3. It was very hot so we decided to spend the day . . . . the beach.
4. Last week a dead whale was washed up . . . . the beach.

"Strolling barefoot along the beach."   *"A whale washed up on the beach."*   *"Burying dad in the sand!"*

sand

Common expressions	Adjective + sand
dig in the sand	hot sand
bury (something) in the sand	dry / wet sand
get sand in (your eyes)	soft sand
(the wind) blows sand into (your eyes)	

1. Verb + sand

Complete the sentences with the correct form of the above verbs:

1. I hate . . . . sand in my shoes! It's so uncomfortable.
2. Our children love . . . . in the sand and making sand castles.
3. I found a set of car keys . . . . in the sand.
4. A sudden gust of wind . . . . sand into our faces.

2. Adjective + sand

Match the halves:

1. The sand was so hot	a. the wet sand to the island.
2. When the tide went out, we walked across	b. the dry sand off my feet.
3. I used a towel to brush	c. the soft sand.
4. My feet kept sinking into	d. it burnt the soles of my feet.

mountain

Adjective + mountain	Common expressions
the highest mountain	climb a mountain
a steep mountain	be surrounded by mountains
Noun + of + mountain	walk in the mountains
the top of a mountain	take a (difficult) route through the mountains
the foot / bottom of a mountain	fall to your death on a mountain
the side of a mountain	
a view of a mountain	

1. Common collocations

Complete the sentences with one word:

1. She was the first American woman to climb Everest, the . . . . mountain in the world.
2. Athens is . . . . by mountains. This makes it very very hot in the middle of summer.
3. K2 in the Himalayas is a very difficult mountain to . . . .
4. It is nearly impossible to climb such a . . . . mountain without special equipment.

Match the halves and note the prepositions that are used with 'mountain':

5. It was a long climb
6. I'm an outdoor person and enjoy walking
7. We took the scenic route
8. Two young climbers fell to their deaths

   a. on Mount Blanc yesterday.
   b. up the mountain, but the view was worth it.
   c. in the mountains at weekends.
   d. through the mountains on our way to Geneva.

2. Noun + of + mountain

Complete the sentences with the above nouns:

1. We camped at the . . . . of the mountain beside a river.
2. My village is situated on the . . . . of a steep mountain, about halfway up.
3. I had a fantastic . . . . of the mountains from my hotel room.
4. We didn't reach the . . . . of the mountain. We had to turn back because of bad weather.

forest

common expressions	
clear a forest	destroy a forest
forests cover (the mountain)	forests shrink
the destruction of the forests	a path through the forest

Common expressions

Complete the sentences with the correct form of a noun or verb from the above expressions:

1. In 1997 huge fires . . . . a large area of tropical rainforest in Borneo.
2. Much of Sweden is . . . . in dense pine forest.
3. Every year millions of acres of forest are . . . . to make the paper for newspaper.
4. There's a . . . . through the middle of the forest, which is quite easy to follow.
5. The world's tropical rainforests have . . . . to almost half the size they were 10 years ago.
6. The Green Party argues that we are all responsible for the . . . . of our forests, and says that we must all play a part in protecting them for future generations.

field

Common expressions

Match the halves:

1. The farmers don't have tractors. They use
2. The village I live in is surrounded by
3. It was a very big farm. There were
4. There were lots of cows

a. green fields.
b. fields of wheat as far as the eye could see.
c. grazing in the fields.
d. oxen to plough their fields.

"A herd of cows grazing in the field."

ground

1. Common expressions

Complete the sentences with the correct preposition:

1. The old man suddenly collapsed and fell . . . . the ground.
2. We lay . . . . the ground and watched the clouds racing across the sky.
3. I had to cross the river using a rope bridge which was about 20 metres . . . . the ground.
4. The miners work about 250 metres . . . . ground.
5. Our school was burned . . . . the ground at the weekend. Police believe the fire was started deliberately.

2. Adjective + ground

Match the halves:

1. The wheels of the car got stuck
2. The ground in the garden is too hard to dig.
3. I had to walk carefully

a. It is frozen solid!
b. over the uneven ground.
c in the soft ground.

Note   Note how we use 'ground' to describe specific places:
Seating for spectators is now compulsory at football grounds in the UK.
There's a Roman burial ground near here, but I'm not sure if anyone famous is buried there.
We found the old lady wandering around the grounds of the hospital.
People are using the waste ground behind the old factory to dump old cars and furniture.

Test 5

| sea | wave | river | island | beach | sand | mountain | forest | field | ground |

1. Identifying the key word

Choose the key word which collocates with these verbs and adjectives:

1.	....	lie on, beautiful, sandy, unspoilt
2.	....	climb, be surrounded by, high, steep
3.	....	live on, sail round, desert, uninhabited
4.	....	dive into, swim in, calm, rough
5.	....	graze in, plough, green
6.	....	frozen, hard, uneven
7.	....	surf, huge, tidal
8.	....	dig in, hot, soft, wet
9.	....	clear, destroy, shrink
10.	....	cross, pollute, long, wide

2. The correct collocation

Choose the correct collocation:

1. The sea was very *rough / strong*. So I didn't really enjoy the ferry crossing.
2. I sat on the beach watching the waves *breaking / falling* on the shore.
3. The River Thames *flows / travels* through the centre of London.
4. These islands *attract / gather* thousands of tourists every year.
5. You'll love the place with its sunny weather and *unspoilt / unused* beaches.
6. I hate it when the wind *blows / throws* sand in your face.
7. It's one of the *highest / tallest* mountains in the area.
8. The world's rainforests are *reducing / shrinking* rapidly.
9. Most modern farmers use tractors to *dig / plough* their fields.

3. Key word quiz

Complete each sentence with the correct key word:

1. The hotel is only 40 metres from the sea and has its own private . . . .
2. It's quite a remote . . . . It takes the ferry about 12 hours to get there.
3. I like going to the swimming pool, but I much prefer swimming in the . . . .
4. We couldn't see the top of the . . . . It was hidden by clouds.
5. We watched the animals grazing in the . . . .
6. Our boat nearly capsized after it was hit by a huge . . . .
7. I think we can cross the . . . . here. It looks quite shallow.
8. The . . . . was very uneven in places, so we had to be careful as we walked.
9. As a child, I loved digging in the . . . . when we went to the beach.

4. Prepositions

Choose the correct preposition to complete these expressions:

1. We spent Sunday *at / in* the beach because the weather was so good.
2. I would like to live in a large house *on / by* the sea.
3. We took the short route *in / through* the mountains on our way to Italy.
4. When I was a boy I lived *in / on* a small island just off the coast of France.
5. It was very stormy with big waves crashing *against / on* the side of our boat.

Section 6

Animals and plants

animal

Common expressions

Match the halves:

1. Some of the animals in the zoo
2. Many people believe that killing animals
3. I think that hunting is cruel to animals, and
4. None of our company's products
5. My father used to take me into the forest
6. Martin's got three dogs and two cats.

a. has been tested on animals.
b. He's a real animal lover.
c. to hunt wild animals.
d. were badly treated.
e. that it should be banned.
f. for sport is wrong.

bird and fish

a bird on its nest   flying away   flapping its wings   swimming   catching a fish

Common expressions

Complete the sentences with the correct form of the above verbs:

1. If most birds . . . . their eggs in spring, how do we get hens to do this all year round?
2. A bird has . . . . its nest in our garage! Come and have a look.
3. I didn't . . . . any fish today. They weren't biting.
4. Many different species of bird . . . . from Europe to Africa for the winter.
5. We always . . . . the birds when the ground is covered by snow.
6. I could see lots of different kinds of colourful fish . . . . under the boat.
7. As we got closer, the bird spread its wings and . . . . away. I'm not sure what kind it was.

Note   Note these noun expressions:
The bird watchers were hoping to spot some woodpeckers in the forest.
A lot of the fish we buy today is produced in fish farms.

pet

Verb + pet

Complete the sentences with the correct form of the above verbs:

1. Believe it or not, rats . . . . very good pets. They sell them in the pet shop.
2. It is important that you teach your children how to . . . . after their pets.
3. One of the conditions of living in this flat is that we can't . . . . pets.
4. You can only have a pet if you agree now that you will . . . . it yourself!

cat and dog

Verb + dog	**Expressions with dog**	**Verb + cat**
look after a dog	take the dog for a walk	cats have kittens
feed the dog	set your dog on someone	cats purr
dogs bite	keep your dog on a lead	cats scratch
dogs bark	Beware of the dog!	cats catch (mice)
dogs attack (people, sheep)	a breed of dog	feed a cat
dogs foul the streets		put the cat out

1. Verb + dog

Complete the sentences with the correct form of the above verbs:

1. I'm . . . . after my neighbour's dog while she's away on holiday.
2. I was . . . . by a dog, and had to go to my doctor to get a tetanus injection.
3. Have you . . . . the dog yet? There's a tin of dog food in the cupboard.
4. The dog next door keeps trying to . . . . my cat, but it never manages to catch it!
5. Dog owners will be fined if they don't clean up when their dogs . . . . the streets.
6. I'm fed up with the dog next door . . . . day and night! We're moving!

2. Common expressions with cat and dog

Match the halves:

1. Dogs must be kept on a lead at all times
2. If you don't leave now,
3. That's a strange-looking dog.
4. The sign on the gate said,
5. Will you take the dog

a. I'll set my dog on you.
b. 'Beware of the Dog.'
c. for a walk, please?
d. while you are in the park.
e. What breed is it?

Complete the sentences with the correct form of the above verbs:

6. My brother says he'll . . . . the cat while we're away.
7. I came home from work to find that my cat had . . . . six kittens!
8. The cat . . . . another mouse last night. That's why it was . . . . so loudly!
9. I usually . . . . the cat out just before I go to bed.
10. Don't worry, Clio's very tame. She won't bite or . . . . you.

Note   Farmers use *sheep dogs*. Blind people use *guide dogs,* which have been specially trained.

plant

Verb + plant	Adjective + plant
a plant grows	a climbing plant
a plant produces (flowers, fruit)	a poisonous plant
a plant is used (in cooking)	a pot plant
water a plant	

1. Verb + plant

Complete the sentences with the correct form of the above verbs:

1. Did you know that a large number of common plants are . . . . to make medicines?
2. Garlic is one plant which . . . . well in a warm climate.
3. It's an attractive plant which . . . . small red berries throughout the autumn.
4. We're going abroad for two weeks. Do you think you could . . . . our plants while we're away in China?

2. Adjective + plant

Match the halves:

1. If there's one kind of pot plant I hate,
2. Climbing plants like ivy may look very nice,
3. Some plants from which we get medicines

a. are very poisonous.
b. it's geraniums.
c. but they can do a lot of damage to buildings.

"Ivy can be a nuisance."

crop

Verb + crop	
plant crops	grow crops
spray crops	harvest crops
(the weather) ruins crops	

Verb + crop

Complete the sentences with the correct form of the above verbs:

1. Unfortunately, 10 days of heavy rain have totally . . . . the crops.
2. Did you know that most farmers . . . . their crops with harmful pesticides?
3. Most of our land is used for . . . . cash crops, like tobacco, cotton and tea.
4. We need to employ extra workers at the beginning of the growing season when we . . . . the crops, and at the end of the season when we . . . . them.

Notes
1. Genetically-modified crops are commonly known as *GM crops*:
   There's an anti-GM-crop demonstration at Hill Farm tomorrow.
2. In example 3, *cash crops* are crops which are grown in order to make money.
3. Crops grow in 'soil':
   Carrots grow well in sandy soil.
4. Notice this example:
   We got a good crop of strawberries this year. It was a good year for them.

flower

Verb + flowers	Adjective + flowers	Common expressions
grow flowers	fresh flowers	a bunch of flowers
pick flowers	artificial flowers	a bouquet of flowers
water flowers	wild flowers	the smell of flowers
send flowers		a flower bed
arrange flowers (in a vase)		

1. Verb + flowers

Complete the sentences with the correct form of the above verbs:

1. I'm going to . . . . more flowers in my garden this year.
2. Don't forget to . . . . the flowers while I'm away.
3. My boyfriend bent down and . . . . a flower, then put it in my hair.
4. Inside the church women were . . . . flowers in large vases.
5. I must remember to . . . . my mother some flowers for her birthday.

2. Adjective + flowers

Complete the sentences with the above adjectives:

1. If I had the money, I'd have . . . . flowers on my desk every day.
2. It's best to visit the island in spring when the fields are full of . . . . flowers.
3. From a distance they looked like real flowers. It was only once you touched them that you realised they were . . . .

3. Noun + of + flowers

Match the halves:

1. I love	a. have the most beautiful flower beds.
2. We'd better get a bunch of flowers	b. the smell of freshly cut flowers.
3. The singer was presented with	c. for your mother.
4. The gardens of the palace	d. a huge bouquet of flowers at the end.

Notes
1. A shop which sells flowers is called a *florist's*. We also use *flower shop*.
2. The difference between a *bunch of flowers* and a *bouquet of flowers* is that a *bouquet* is more formal, elaborate, and more expensive.

grass

Expressions with grass			
long / short grass	cut / mow the grass	lie on the grass	keep off the grass

Expressions with grass

Complete the sentences with one word in each space:

1. The grass is getting too . . . . It's time it was . . . .
2. . . . . off the grass! You're not allowed to walk or lie on it.
3. We . . . . on the grass all afternoon, reading and sunbathing.

Note
The area of grass around a house is called a *lawn*. You cut it with a *lawnmower*.
Dad's very proud of his lawn.

tree

Verb + tree	Common expressions
climb a tree	crash into a tree
plant a tree	you fall out of a tree
cut down a tree	(leaves) fall off a tree
trees grow	take cover under / beneath a tree
trees are blown down	(the street) is lined with trees.

1. Verb + tree

Complete the sentences with the correct form of the above verbs:

1. We had to dig quite a big hole before we were able to . . . . the apple tree.
2. As a kid, I loved . . . . trees. Luckily, I never fell out of one.
3. Some of these trees can . . . . up to 30 metres in height.
4. Thousands of trees were . . . . down in the great storm last month.
5. I don't know why they . . . . down so many trees in the park. There's hardly any left.

2. Common expressions

Complete the sentences with the correct preposition:

1. By the end of November, all the leaves had fallen . . . . the trees.
2. Many of the famous streets in Paris are lined . . . . trees.
3. The bus left the road and crashed . . . . a tree.
4. When the rain started, we took cover . . . . a huge oak tree.

Notes
1. Note these adjective collocations:
   A fallen tree blocked the path and we had to climb over it.
   The car was crushed by a falling tree.
2. A 'Christmas tree' is a real or artificial tree people have in their house at Christmas:
   We haven't decorated our Christmas tree yet.
3. We use the verb 'shed' to describe a tree losing its leaves:
   In autumn many trees shed their leaves.
4. Trees are either *deciduous* (oak, birch, elm etc) or *coniferous* (pine, spruce, larch).

garden

common expressions		
work in the garden	dig the garden	a tidy / overgrown garden

Common expressions

Complete the sentences with the correct form of the verb or adjective:

1. My mother gets a lot of satisfaction from . . . . in the garden.
2. It should be a . . . . garden! He spends most of his life in it. I never see him!
3. . . . . the garden is hard work, but it's also good exercise.
4. The garden has been neglected all year and it's now . . . . The grass actually comes up to your waist!

Note
If you 'do' the garden, you work in it:
Do you do the garden yourself or do you get someone to do it for you?

fence

Verb + fence	Adjective + fence
climb over a fence	the garden fence
put up a fence	a high / low fence
mend a fence	an electrified fence
	a barbed-wire fence

1. Verb + fence

Complete the sentences with the correct form of the above verbs:

1. The neighbour's son often . . . . over the fence into our garden to get his ball back.
2. It took me two days to . . . . up a new fence in the back garden after it fell down in the high winds last week.
3. I've got to . . . . our fence this weekend. I hit it with my car!

2. Adjective + fence

Match the halves:

1. We put up a barbed-wire fence
2. Our garden fence is too high,
3. Our garden fence needs
4. The field next to us has an electrified fence

a. a new coat of paint.
b. to keep the cows from escaping.
c. for children to climb over.
d. to stop sheep getting into our garden.

"It's time I painted my fence."

"Someone's left the gate open!"

gate

Common expressions		
open / shut a gate	leave the gate (wide) open	the garden gate
the factory gates	the school gates	

Common expressions

Complete the sentences with one word:

1. The . . . . gates open at 7.30 every morning, but most children don't arrive till 8.30.
2. Someone had . . . . the gate wide open and the sheep had managed to get out onto the main road.
3. While walking in the countryside, please remember to . . . . all gates behind you.
4. When the workers turned up this morning, the . . . . gates were closed.
5. Our . . . . gate leads out onto the open fields at the back of our house.

Test 6

animal	bird	fish	pet	cat	dog	plant	crop	flower	grass	tree	garden	fence	gate

1. Identifying the key word

Choose the key word which collocates with these verbs, adjectives and nouns:

1. . . . .   pick, wild, water, artificial
2. . . . .   catch mice, have kittens, scratch
3. . . . .   climb, cut down, fall out of
4. . . . .   hunt, kill, treat badly, wild
5. . . . .   cut, keep off, long
6. . . . .   fly, migrate, build nests
7. . . . .   dig, tidy, overgrown
8. . . . .   bite, attack sheep, foul streets
9. . . . .   climb over, mend, put up
10. . . . .   grow, water, climbing, pot

2. The correct collocation

Choose the correct collocation:

1. I can't understand people who *deal with* / *treat* animals badly.
2. Most birds *have* / *lay* their eggs in spring.
3. Rabbits *form* / *make* good pets.
4. I was *bitten* / *cut* on the leg when I was attacked by a large dog.
5. Our cat *had* / *made* four kittens last week.
6. It's a climbing plant which *makes* / *produces* large red flowers.
7. I'll just go into the garden and *pick* / *pull* some flowers.
8. The leaves are beginning to *go off* / *fall off* the trees.

3. Key word quiz

Complete each sentence with the correct key word:

1. The . . . . is getting long. We'll need to cut it this weekend.
2. The landlord says we're not allowed to keep any kind of . . . . in the flat.
3. Keep your . . . . on a lead so that it doesn't chase the sheep.
4. A large . . . . flew out of the tree as I walked towards it.
5. I'm a vegetarian because I feel it is wrong to kill . . . .
6. I bought my wife a large bunch of . . . . on her birthday.
7. The . . . . at the back of the house is overgrown.
8. Someone's left the garden . . . . wide open again!
9. No, I won't pick up your . . . . It scratched me last time I tried!
10. My son loves climbing . . . . I just hope he doesn't fall out of one of them.

4. Prepositions

Choose the correct preposition to complete these expressions:

1. I don't think I can climb *over* / *up* that fence. It's too high.
2. I think that testing drugs *on* / *with* animals is cruel and should be banned.
3. Please keep *away from* / *off* the grass.
4. Farmers spray their crops *with* / *by* pesticides to stop insects eating them.
5. I'll set my dog *at* / *on* you if you come any closer.
6. The main streets of the city are lined *in* / *with* trees.

Section 7

Transport

car

Verb + car	Adjective + car	Car + noun
drive a car	a luxury car	a car alarm
hire a car	a reliable car	a car accident
park a car	an economical car	a car park
get into / out of a car	a spacious car	your car keys
cars start	a sports car	
cars crash		
cars skid		
cars break down		

"Well, it may not be very economical, but it's reliable, comfortable, and very fast!"

1. Verb + car

Complete the sentences with the correct form of the above verbs:

1. He . . . . into the car and drove off towards the motorway.
2. I'm afraid we have a problem. I can't remember where I . . . . the car!
3. Don't ask dad if you can use his car. He never lets anyone else . . . . it.
4. Mike . . . . his mum's car. He ran into the back of a bus outside the cinema.
5. The car wouldn't . . . . , so we had to take a bus.
6. My car . . . . down on the way to work, so I was late for an important meeting.
7. The car . . . . when I braked suddenly. At least we didn't crash!
8. We usually . . . . a car when we go on holiday. You can see a lot more that way.

2. Adjective + car

Complete the sentences with the above adjectives:

1. The car I have just now is very . . . . It does about 20 kilometres to the litre!
2. The sales of . . . . cars like Porsche and Rolls Royce increased sharply last year.
3. It's a . . . . car with lots of room. It seats five adults comfortably.
4. My new car is certainly more . . . . The last one was never out of the garage!
5. I used to have a really fast open-topped . . . . car when I was younger, but it's not very practical in the winter!

3. Car + noun

Complete the sentences with the above nouns:

1. Many of the people badly injured in car . . . . weren't wearing seat belts.
2. I've lost my car . . . . and I can't find them anywhere.
3. My neighbour's car . . . . went off at 2am and woke the whole street up!
4. We didn't stop to visit the castle because the car . . . . was full!

bus

Verb + bus	Noun + bus
get on / off a bus	a bus stop
miss / catch a bus	a bus timetable
run for a bus	the bus fare
wait for a bus	the bus service
buses stop	
the bus leaves (for the airport)	

1. Verb + bus

Complete the sentences with the correct form of the above verbs:

1. I . . . . the last bus and had to walk home.
2. I had to . . . . over an hour for a bus, and then three arrived at the same time!
3. The best bus to get is the 22. It . . . . right outside the school.
4. I get the bus to work. I usually . . . . the express bus to Valencia at 8am.
5. Please wait until the bus stops before you . . . . off.
6. Can you tell me what time the next bus . . . . for the city centre?
7. I got up late this morning and had to . . . . for the bus. I just managed to get it.

2. Bus + noun

Complete the sentences with the above nouns:

1. Copenhagen has an excellent bus . . . . There are regular buses to the city centre.
2. I'll buy the tickets. You check the bus . . . . and find out when the next one leaves.
3. He says he walked to the interview because he couldn't afford the bus . . . .
4. I stood at the bus . . . . for over half an hour before a bus came along.

Note   Note these expressions:
It's about 20 minutes away by bus. But the bus service is very good.
Excuse me, is this the bus to Oxford?
I like to sit on the top deck of the bus. You get a better view.

petrol

Common expressions	
fill up with petrol	run out of petrol
be out of petrol	(the car) uses / runs on petrol
a tankful of petrol	the price of petrol

Common expressions

Match the halves:

1. Unfortunately, we ran out of petrol	a. fill up at the next station.
2. Does your car run on petrol or	b. go on a tankful of petrol?
3. We're nearly out of petrol. I'll have to	c. in the middle of nowhere.
4. The price of petrol is	d. unleaded petrol.
5. Do you know how far your car can	e. diesel?
6. Most modern cars use	f. going up again.

plane

Verb + plane

board a plane

fly a plane

planes crash

planes are diverted

catch a plane

planes take off / land

planes are delayed

Verb + plane

Complete the sentences with the correct form of the above verbs:

1. When I heard my mother was ill, I drove to the airport and . . . . the first plane home.
2. I'd love to be able to . . . . a plane.
3. It was minus 5 degrees when we . . . . the plane in Moscow, but it was plus 33 when we stepped off the plane in Singapore!
4. My son likes going to the airport to watch the planes take off and . . . .
5. A plane carrying 120 passengers has . . . . into a mountain in the north of the country.
6. The plane's been . . . . by five hours. It is now expected to arrive at 12pm.
7. Our plane was . . . . to Bristol airport because there was heavy fog at Cardiff. We had to finish our journey by coach.

Note   Note these expressions:
I'm a little nervous. I've never flown in such a small plane before.
What time does Pete's plane get in? (arrive)

airport

Verb + airport

build an airport

close an airport

depart from an airport

circle an airport

arrive at / get to the airport

be stranded at the airport

Verb + airport

Complete the sentences with the correct form of the above verbs:

1. Heavy snow has . . . . several airports in the south of the country.
2. Our airports are now heavily congested. It's clear that the government needs to . . . . some new airports.
3. Heathrow was very busy and we had to . . . . the airport, waiting for a landing slot.

Complete the sentences with the correct preposition:

4. It's an early morning flight. It departs . . . . Orly Airport at 6am.
5. We were stranded . . . . the airport for 48 hours after the air traffic controllers went on strike.
6. We got . . . . the airport with just 15 minutes to spare.

Notes   1. Note the expression:
       My parents saw me off at the airport. (came with me to say goodbye)
    2. Note these noun + preposition + airport expressions:
       The hotel is within easy reach of the airport.
       Just follow the signs for the airport.

train

Verb + train	**Common expressions**
catch / miss the train	train ticket
change trains	direct train
board / get on a train	express train
get off a train	train times
trains run late	train timetable
trains depart / leave (on time)	train arrival and departure times
trains travel (fast, slow, at 100 kph)	earlier / later train

1. Verb + train

Complete the sentences with the correct form of the above verbs:

1. You'd better hurry or you'll . . . . the train.
2. There are no direct trains to Paris from here. You have to . . . . trains at Lyons.
3. I'm afraid I can't stay much longer. I have a train to . . . .
4. Jill! Don't try to . . . . off the train until it has stopped.
5. Nobody . . . . on the train at Chester. The station was completely empty.

Match the halves:

6. All our trains are running late   a. at over 200 kph.
7. Some high speed trains travel   b. from platform 3.
8. The train to Grantham will leave   c. because of the snow.

2. Preposition focus

Complete the sentences with at, by, from, in, on or to:

1. Can I catch the express train . . . . Madrid from this station?
2. Excuse me. When does the overnight train from Hamburg get . . . . ?
   > I think it's due . . . . at 6am.
3. My next-door neighbour travels . . . . the same train as me to work every day.
4. I never take the car to work. It's actually quicker . . . . train.

3. Common expressions

Match the halves:

1. I booked the train tickets on the internet,   a. let's get the earlier train.
2. Is it a direct train   b. The No 8515 to Bordeaux leaves at 22.40.
3. Just to be on the safe side,   c. but we'll have to pick them up at the station.
4. I'm sure I can download   d. or do we have to change?
5. I think we should get a later train.   e. the train timetable.

Notes
1. The illustration at the top of this page is of a *goods train* – one that carries *goods* not *passengers*.
2. Overnight trains with beds are called *sleepers*:
   I'm getting the sleeper from London to Inverness tonight.
   Note that we call the train 'the sleeper' – not 'the sleeper train'.

taxi

Verb + taxi	Taxi + noun
take a taxi (to work)	a taxi driver
drive a taxi	a taxi rank
wait for a taxi	a taxi ride
call a taxi	the taxi fare
share a taxi	
jump into a taxi	

1. Verb + taxi

Complete the sentences with the correct form of the above verbs:

1. My dad's a teacher, but he . . . . a taxi at the weekends to make some extra money.
2. I'd . . . . a taxi if I were you. It'll be much quicker than the bus.
3. If the four of us . . . . a taxi, it'll be almost as cheap as going by bus.
4. I . . . . into a taxi outside the hotel and told the driver to take me to the airport.
5. I'll get my secretary to . . . . you a taxi.
6. How long did you have to . . . . for a taxi?

2. Taxi + noun

Complete the sentences with the above nouns:

1. It's just a short taxi . . . . from the airport to my house. It shouldn't cost much.
2. If you want to know anything about a city, just ask a taxi . . . . !
3. How much is the taxi . . . . to the airport?
4. There's a taxi . . . . outside the station, so you'll have no problems getting a taxi.

Note   If you *hail a taxi*, you stand in the street and stop one which is available.

ferry

Verb + ferry	Ferry + noun
board a ferry	a ferry crossing
catch / take a ferry	a ferry terminal
cross by ferry	
ferries sail	
ferries link / connect (places, islands)	

Common collocations

Complete the sentences with one word:

1. There isn't a bridge across the river – you have to . . . . by ferry.
2. When you arrive at the ferry . . . . , someone will tell you where to park.
3. There are regular ferry . . . . from Calais to Dover.
4. A daily ferry . . . . the islands to the mainland.
5. We . . . . the overnight ferry from Harwich to Rotterdam.
6. You won't be allowed to . . . . the ferry until about half an hour before it sails.
7. The ferry won't . . . . if the weather is bad.

bike

Verb + bike	Common expressions
ride a bike	have a go on someone's bike
get on / off your bike	go for a ride on your bike
fall off your bike	lean your bike against (a wall)
hire a bike	chain your bike to (a gate)
knock somebody off their bike	your bike has a puncture

1. Verb + bike

Complete the sentences with the correct form of the above verbs:

1. Unfortunately, I . . . . off my bike and broke my arm in two places.
2. I couldn't . . . . on my dad's bike. It was too big for me.
3. My younger brother is learning to . . . . a bike at the moment.
4. I have to . . . . off my bike and push it up a steep hill to get to school.
5. I nearly had an accident today. Some idiot in a car almost . . . . me off my bike!
6. I always . . . . a bike when I'm on holiday. It's the best way to get around.

2. Common expressions

Match the halves:

1. At night I chain my bike to a lamppost	a. before I went into the shop.
2. I had to push my bike home from school today.	b. for a ride on his bike.
3. Neil's not in. He's gone	c. on your new bike?
4. Can I have a go	d. so that nobody will steal it.
5. I leant my bike against the wall	e. It had a puncture in the front wheel.

lorry

Common expressions	
load / unload a lorry	drive a lorry
lorries carry things	lorries deliver things
lorries overturn	a heavy lorry

Common expressions

Complete the sentences with the correct form of the above verbs:

1. You need a special licence to . . . . a lorry in most countries.
2. Fresh bread and milk are . . . . by lorry every morning before the shop opens.
3. . . . . the lorry was hard work. I'm exhausted.
4. The lorry in front of us was . . . . sheep.
5. A lorry carrying coal . . . . on the main road yesterday. It blocked the main road for nearly six hours.

Note   Note these expressions:
Heavy lorries can't cross the old bridge. They have to use the tunnel.
The road was closed after a lorry shed its load. (dropped what it was carrying)
A lorry ran into the back of me at the traffic lights. (hit my car at the back)

Test 7

car	bus	petrol	plane	airport	train	taxi	ferry	bike	lorry

1. Identifying the key word

Choose the key word which collocates with these verbs:

1. . . . .   run for, get on, get off, miss
2. . . . .   fall off, get on, hire, ride
3. . . . .   board, sail, take
4. . . . .   get into, get out of, hire, park
5. . . . .   drive, load, carry (things)
6. . . . .   express, catch, change, get on, miss
7. . . . .   call, drive, hail, share
8. . . . .   be stuck at, circle, close
9. . . . .   board, catch, crash, fly
10. . . . .   fill up with, run on, price of

2. The correct collocation

Choose the correct collocation:

1. I was sixteen before I learned to *drive / ride* a bike.
2. Don't *get off / get out of* the bus while it is moving.
3. Quite a few people got off at the station but no one *boarded / got into* the train.
4. Let me know when you're leaving and I'll *call / ring* you a taxi.
5. There's a taxi *station / rank* just outside the hotel.

3. Key word quiz

Complete each sentence with the correct key word:

1. I can't use my . . . . It's got a puncture.
2. There's no bridge or air link to the island, so you'll have to cross by . . . .
3. There's a . . . . stop just outside my house.
4. There's no direct rail link. You'll have to change . . . . at Oxford.
5. Has anyone seem my . . . . keys?
6. It took us nearly an hour to unload the crates of milk from the . . . .
7. This is the first time I've flown in such a huge . . . .
8. I saved money by sharing a . . . . from the airport with two other tourists.
9. The waiting room at the railway . . . . was very crowded.

4. Prepositions

Choose the correct preposition to complete these expressions:

1. I think he's gone out for a ride *in / on* his bike.
2. The island can only be reached *by / with* ferry.
3. I had to brake suddenly when a bus pulled *away / out* in front of me.
4. A heavy lorry ran *into / up* the back of the bus.
5. Their plane lands *at / on* Heathrow in about half an hour.
6. I waited nearly an hour before a taxi came *along / in*.
7. Her train's due *in / on* at 2.30 this afternoon.
8. I can drop you *at / to* the station on my way to work.

Section 8

Travel

road

Verb + road	Adjective + road	Road + noun
cross the road	a busy road	a road accident
dig up the road	a clear road	a road sign
follow the road	an icy road	road safety
build roads	a wide / narrow road	
block the road	the main road	
	the wrong road	

1. Verb + road

Complete the sentences with the correct form of the above verbs:

1. . . . . the main road till you come to a cinema. Then turn right.
2. It's easier to . . . . the road here – at the lights.
3. Some road workers are . . . . up the road outside my house, so I can't get my car back into the garage.
4. Thousands of people were late for work today when angry farmers . . . . the roads into the city with their tractors.
5. I think the only way to solve the traffic problems in this country is for the government to . . . . more roads.

2. Adjective + road

Complete the sentences with the above adjectives:

1. We took the . . . . road and lost our way. We eventually had to ask a policeman for directions.
2. The road into town is very . . . . on weekdays, but quite quiet at the weekends.
3. Let's wait until the roads are . . . . , then we'll leave. I hate driving in heavy traffic.
4. Some of the country roads were very . . . . Sometimes, there was only enough room for one car.
5. The roads are . . . . this morning, so take care when you are driving to work.
6. When we reached the city we left the . . . . road and turned into a side road, hoping to find somewhere to park.

3. Road + noun

Complete the sentences with the above nouns:

1. We had lessons in road . . . . when we were at primary school.
2. There were no road . . . . at the junction, so I didn't know which turning to take.
3. Speeding is the main cause of road . . . .

4. Preposition focus

Match the halves:

1. The journey takes about six hours	a. at the side of the road, outside the bank.
2. I parked the car	b. by road, or one hour by air.
3. I stopped because a cow was standing	c. across the road when she was knocked down.
4. My friend Ashti lives about 100 metres	d. on the roads these days.
5. I think there are too many cars	e. off the main road. You can't miss it.
6. The old woman was walking	f. in the middle of the road.
7. The cinema is just	g. down the road from me in an old cottage.

journey

"It's been a long and tiring journey, but we're here at last!"

1. Verb + journey

Complete the sentences with the correct form of the above verbs:

1. My journey to school . . . . from 40 minutes to an hour, depending on the traffic.
2. Why do so many car drivers . . . . the journey to work alone?
3. Our train broke down and we had to . . . . the journey by coach.
4. Harry . . . . off on his journey across Asia about a month ago, but nobody has heard from him yet.
5. It's always a good idea to . . . . a long car journey. It reduces the risk of having an accident.

2. Adjective + journey

Complete the sentences with the above adjectives:

1. Have a . . . . journey. We hope to see you again soon.
2. Our house is only a . . . . journey from the airport. It's only a five-minute drive away.
3. You'd better save some money for the . . . . journey.
4. The journey home was very . . . . The roads were so busy I had to concentrate all the time.
5. It's quite a . . . . journey. It takes about 12 hours by bus or 9 by train.
6. We arrived in Oslo after an . . . . journey – no delays, no problems whatsoever.
7. We had an . . . . journey. First, there was heavy rain and then the car broke down.

Notes

1. Note these common expressions:
   How was the journey home?
   We're still in touch with friends we made on the journey back from Stockholm.
   The journey to work in the rush-hour is a nightmare.
   The last stage / leg of the journey was by helicopter.

2. Note the expression 'journey time':
   Bad weather could add another hour to your journey time.
   These new trains are much faster. They are going to cut an hour off the journey time.

driver

Verb + driver	Adjective + driver
drivers speed	a drunk driver
drivers lose control	a good / safe driver
drivers are killed	a learner driver
drivers turn (left)	an injured driver

1. Verb + driver

Match the halves:

1. Drivers who are caught speeding   a. without indicating.
2. The driver turned right   b. on the icy road, and crashed into a bus shelter.
3. The driver of the bus was killed   c. will receive a heavy fine.
4. The driver lost control of the vehicle   d. outright in the accident.

2. Adjective + driver

Complete the sentences with the correct form of the above adjectives:

1. It is a myth that men are . . . . drivers than women.
2. . . . . drivers are a danger to everyone.
3. Fire-fighters helped free the . . . . driver from the wreckage of the truck.
4. I'm still a . . . . driver. I haven't passed my test yet.

Notes   1. We talk about *car, bus, taxi, truck* and *train drivers*.
      A back seat driver is an annoying person who is always telling the driver what to do.
      A hit-and-run driver is one who causes an accident, then drives away.
   2. Note these expressions with 'driving':
      He was charged with causing death by dangerous driving.
      He was found guilty of reckless driving and disqualified from driving for 6 months.
      He was arrested for driving under the influence of alcohol at the time of the accident.

licence

Verb + licence	
hold a licence	lose your licence
see your licence	licences are endorsed

Verb + licence

Complete the sentences with the correct form of the above verbs:

1. He was caught drunk driving and has . . . . his driving licence for two years.
2. All applicants for the job must . . . . a driving licence.
3. She was fined £300 for speeding, and her licence was . . . .
4. I was pulled over by a patrol car and a police officer asked to . . . . my licence.

Notes   1. Note the following expression:
      I've got a clean driving licence. (I have committed no driving offences.)
   2. In the UK you receive *three penalty points on your licence* if you are caught speeding. When you have 12 penalty points, you lose your licence.

tourist

Verb + tourist	Tourist + noun
attract tourists	a tourist attraction
scare away tourists	a (popular) tourist destination
tourists arrive	a tourist office
tourists visit (a country)	a tourist visa
rob tourists	the tourist industry
	the tourist season

1. Verb + tourist

Complete the sentences with the correct form of the above verbs:

1. A number of tourists have been . . . . recently. Don't carry cash around with you.
2. The number of American tourists who . . . . Europe has decreased since 2001.
3. The recent bomb attacks on hotels have . . . . away the tourists.
4. Millions of British tourists . . . . in Spain every July and August.
5. Tourists are . . . . to the islands by the great beaches and fantastic weather.

2. Tourist + noun

Match the halves:

1. This course prepares students for jobs in	a. a tourist visa.
2. You'll get leaflets about places to visit from	b. the world's top tourist destinations.
3. The city map shows all	c. the tourist season is over.
4. Disneyland is one of	d. the tourist office.
5. To go on holiday to China, I had to get	e. the tourist industry.
6. The town's pretty quiet in winter when	f. the major tourist attractions.

Notes
1. Note this way of talking about a lot of tourists:
   Every summer the town is invaded by tourists.
2. Note these expressions:
   This hotel is very popular with tourists.
   Many tourists are worried they'll get ripped off. (pay far too much for something)

tour

Adjective + tour	
a coach tour	a guided tour
a package tour	a (five-day) tour

Adjective + tour

Complete the sentences with the above adjectives:

1. Last year I went on an eight- . . . . walking tour in the French Alps.
2. I never go on . . . . tours. I always feel sick on buses.
3. We went on a . . . . tour of Rome on an open-top bus.
4. . . . . tours are still the cheapest way of visiting a country.

Note   Note the expression:
I work as a tour guide during my holidays from university.

ticket

Verb + ticket	Adjective + ticket
buy a ticket	a lottery ticket
issue (you) with a ticket	a parking ticket
lose a ticket	a plane ticket
sell a ticket	a season ticket

1. Verb + ticket

Complete the sentences with the correct form of the above verbs:

1. I . . . . my ticket and they wouldn't let me on the plane.
2. The organisers have already . . . . 25,000 tickets for next month's exhibition.
3. In my country, you need to . . . . a ticket from a machine or a shop before you get on the bus. The driver can't . . . . you with a ticket – he only drives the bus.

2. Adjective + ticket

Complete the sentences with the above adjectives:

1. I left my car on double yellow lines and got another . . . . ticket!
2. The first prize was a . . . . ticket – a return flight to New York.
3. I always buy a . . . . ticket at the weekend. I still dream of winning millions one day.
4. If you go to a lot of football matches, you'll save money if you buy a . . . . ticket.

Note   We talk about *air, rail, plane* and *bus tickets; cinema, theatre* and *concert tickets.*

queue

Verb + queue	
be in a queue	stand in a queue
join a queue	jump the queue
the queue stretched for (half a mile)	

Verb + queue

Complete the sentences with the correct form of the above verbs:

1. If you want tickets for the ferry, you'll have to . . . . the queue at the ticket office.
2. I was . . . . in the bus queue when two boys pushed in front of me.
3. The queue at the bus stop . . . . down the road and round the corner.
4. Excuse me, ... you in the queue?
5. Just because you have to get home quickly doesn't mean you can . . . . the queue – so get to the back of the queue and wait in line like everyone else!

seat

Verb + seat	Adjective + seat	Common expressions
give up your seat	a back seat	get up from your seat
save someone a seat	an empty seat	show someone to their seat
leave your seat	a good seat	hold onto the seat
reserve a seat	a reclining seat	climb into your seat
the seat is taken	a(n) (un)comfortable seat	someone is in your seat
	a(n) aisle / window seat	

1. Verb + seat

Complete the sentences with the correct form of the above verbs:

1. The 8 o'clock is a very busy train, so it's a good idea to . . . . a seat.
2. . . . . me a seat if you get there before me.
3. Excuse me. Is this seat free or has it been . . . . ?
4. I . . . . up my seat on the bus to a pregnant woman.
5. Please do not . . . . your seat until the plane has come to a complete standstill and the seatbelt sign has been switched off.

2. Adjective + seat

Complete the sentences with the above adjectives:

1. There were no . . . . seats left in the hall when I arrived. There was standing room only.
2. I always feel sick in the . . . . seat of a car. That's why I prefer to sit in the passenger seat.
3. On a plane I prefer an . . . . seat to a window seat. It's easier to get in and out.
4. We arrived early at the concert to be sure of getting a . . . . seat.
5. They were the most . . . . seats I've ever sat in. They were incredibly small and very hard.
6. We travelled by luxury coach with . . . . seats. You could lie back and sleep quite comfortably.

3. Common expressions

Match the halves:

1. A member of the cabin crew
2. He climbed into the driver's seat
3. My ticket says 27G,
4. I had to hold onto my seat

a. as the bus went round round the corner.
b. but there's already someone in that seat.
c. and drove off.
d. showed us to our seats.

Notes
1. If you ask someone to *take a seat*, you are asking them politely to sit down:
   Please take a seat. Mr Smith will be with you in a few minutes.
2. Note the expression:
   Make sure your seat is in the upright position for landing. (on a plane)
3. Note these expressions with 'seatbelt':
   Remember to wear your seatbelt in the car.
   Please fasten your seatbelt for take-off.
   I hate to think what could have happened if we hadn't been wearing seatbelts.

Test 8

| road | journey | driver | licence | tourist | tour | ticket | queue | seat |

1. Identifying the key word

Choose the key word which collocates with these verbs, adjectives and nouns:

1. .... leave, reserve, aisle, empty
2. .... hold, lose, be endorsed
3. .... block, cross, busy, icy
4. .... buy, issue, lottery, plane
5. .... speed, drunk, safe
6. .... visit, attraction, destination
7. .... break, make, set off on, long
8. .... join, jump, stand in
9. .... coach, guided, package

2. The correct collocation

Choose the correct collocation:

1. We'll drive home once the roads are *clear / open*. I hate driving in heavy traffic.
2. Too many people today *do / make* the journey to work by car.
3. My brother's still a *learner / trainee* driver, but he's going to sit his test next month.
4. I've got a *clean / clear* licence. I've never been fined for speeding or any other driving offence.
5. Turkey is a very popular tourist *destination / place* for British tourists.
6. The queue for tickets *ran / stretched* right round the corner.
7. Is the seat next to you free or is it *saved / taken*?

3. Key word quiz

Complete each sentence with the correct key word:

1. The .... lost control of the car and it hit a wall.
2. If your .... is a long one, make sure you break it at regular intervals.
3. The Tower of London is visited by nearly a million .... every year.
4. I got a parking .... for stopping on some double yellow lines.
5. He lost his .... after he killed a child while driving carelessly.
6. Make sure you look both ways before crossing the ....
7. I had to stand at the back of the hall. There wasn't an empty .... anywhere.
8. I joined a long .... of people standing outside the box office.
9. I think the best way to see a city is to go on a guided ....

4. Prepositions

Choose the correct preposition to complete these expressions:

1. There are too many cars *in / on* the roads nowadays.
2. Many tourists are attracted *into / to* the city by its beautiful buildings.
3. Could you keep my place *in / on* the queue while I go to the toilet?
4. When are you setting off *for / on* your journey round the world?
5. Call into our office and we will issue you *for / with* a replacement ticket.
6. He was driving so fast I had to hold *onto / to* my seat.

Section 9

Meals and eating out

breakfast

Verb + breakfast	Adjective + breakfast	Common expressions
have breakfast	an enormous breakfast	have (cereal) for breakfast
make breakfast	a light breakfast	discuss (work) over breakfast
skip breakfast	a cooked breakfast	go without breakfast
	a continental breakfast	(swim) before breakfast

1. Verb and adjective collocations

Complete the sentences with the correct form of the above adjectives or verbs:

1. It's not a good idea to . . . . breakfast. It's the most important meal of the day.
2. I like to . . . . breakfast in bed on Sundays.
3. I don't know how he managed lunch after the . . . . breakfast he had this morning!
4. I always have a fairly . . . . breakfast – just a . . . . breakfast of coffee and a croissant. I can't eat a . . . . breakfast of bacon and eggs!
5. Could you get the kids dressed while I . . . . breakfast?

2. Common expressions:

Match the halves:

1. I went for a swim in the hotel pool	a. over a working breakfast.
2. We chatted about business	b. for breakfast.
3. I had cereal and toast	c. without breakfast.
4. I often go to work	d. before breakfast.

Note   Note these expressions
Bed and breakfast is 23 Euros.
Could you wash up the breakfast things? (plate, cups etc)

lunch

Adjective + lunch	Common expressions
a (three)-course lunch	be free for lunch
an early / a late lunch	meet someone for lunch
a light lunch	have a (sandwich) for lunch
a packed lunch	be closed for lunch
a working lunch	get (an hour) for lunch
Sunday lunch	break for lunch
	(the bank) is closed for lunch

1. Adjective + lunch

Complete the sentences with the above adjectives:

1. I only had a . . . . lunch. I wasn't very hungry.
2. The meeting will break for a short . . . . lunch around midday.
3. I just had the two- . . . . lunch. I didn't feel like dessert.
4. It's an all-day trip so bring a . . . . lunch with you.
5. The British traditionally have roast beef for . . . . lunch.
6. We had an . . . . lunch, so that we could spend the whole afternoon shopping.

2. Common expressions:

Match the halves:

1. I said I'd meet him for lunch if
2. Are you free
3. At work we're only allowed
4. The post office is closed for lunch
5. Nowadays a lot of people just
6. We plan to

a. for lunch today?
b. I could get away.
c. between 12.30 and 1.30.
d. half an hour for lunch.
e. break for lunch around 12.
f. have a sandwich for lunch.

"She's late for lunch – again!"

dinner

Verb + dinner	Verb + for + dinner
have dinner	go out for dinner
prepare / cook dinner	dress for dinner
invite (you) to dinner	pay for dinner
(you) come to dinner	have (chicken) for dinner
	take (her) out for dinner

1. Verb + dinner

Complete the sentences with the correct form of the above verbs:

1. Anne and Tom are in the kitchen . . . . dinner.
2. What time do you usually . . . . dinner? I usually eat around six.
3. She's such a nice person. Let's . . . . her to dinner next Saturday.
4. Guess who's . . . . to dinner? Her new boyfriend!

2. Verb + for + dinner

Match the halves:

1. Is your company paying for dinner?
2. My parents would like to take us out for dinner.
3. Do you ever dress for dinner?
4. How about going out for dinner tonight?
5. What are you having for dinner tonight?

a. I don't think we can afford it.
b. Only when we stay at hotels.
c. Fish again!
d. I certainly hope so.
e. Do you want to go?

Notes

1. Note these types of dinner:
   Andrew took me for a romantic dinner by candlelight on Friday night.
   The restaurant is offering a three-course dinner for only £5.00. That's fantastic value!

2. Note these *dinner + noun* expressions:
   Let's throw a dinner party for her when she gets home next week.
   His after-dinner speech was very amusing.

3. Note these expressions:
   Is dinner ready yet? I'm absolutely starving!
   Save me some dinner, and I'll have it when I get in.
   Eat up all your dinner, and you can have some chocolate.

restaurant

Verb + restaurant	**Adjective + restaurant**	**Noun + of + restaurant**
work in a restaurant	a (Chinese) restaurant	a chain of restaurants
try out a (new) restaurant	an expensive restaurant	a (quiet) corner of the . . .
recommend a restaurant	a cheap restaurant	the non-smoking section of
run a restaurant	the restaurant is fully booked	the restaurant
restaurants serve food		

1. Verb + restaurant

Complete the sentences with the correct form of the above verbs:

1. We're going to . . . . out that new Chinese restaurant in Walton Road tonight. It got a really good review in the paper last week.
2. The hotel has a restaurant which . . . . good food all day.
3. She's . . . . in a restaurant at the moment, but she's a teacher by profession. I don't understand why!
4. Can you . . . . a good restaurant near here? I really like Mexican food, but if there's no Mexican restaurant, Italian will do.
5. My uncle . . . . a busy restaurant in the centre of town and he works all hours.

2. Adjective + restaurant

Complete the sentences with the above adjectives:

1. My boss took me out for a five-course dinner in an . . . . restaurant. It cost a fortune! But the food was out of this world!
2. Do you know any good . . . . restaurants round here? I'm in the mood for a pizza.
3. The area round the university is full of . . . . restaurants for students.
4. Unfortunately, the Apollo restaurant was . . . . at lunchtime, so we went in the evening instead.

3. Noun + preposition + restaurant

Match the halves:

1. She owns a successful
2. We found a table in a
3. We ate in the non-smoking

   a. section of the restaurant.
   b. chain of restaurants in England and Wales.
   c. quiet corner of the restaurant.

Notes

1. Note the verbs we use to describe starting up a restaurant:
   I see they're opening a new seafood restaurant next door.
   He set up a vegetarian restaurant with his brother-in-law.
   Fast-food restaurants are shooting / springing up everywhere.
2. Note these common expressions:
   The restaurant is under new management.
   The restaurant is famous for its pasta / curries / French cuisine.
3. If you want to recommend a restaurant to someone, here are some ways of doing so:
   It's got a very good reputation.
   It gets a very good name.
   It's famous for its seafood.
4. If a restaurant is *licensed,* it serves alcohol.
5. Restaurants which serve food to take away, are often called *fast-food restaurants:*
   No wonder so many children are fat! They eat nothing but take-aways from fast-food restaurants!

waiter / waitress

Common expressions	**Adjective + waiter**
work as a waiter	a friendly waiter
call the waiter	a rude waiter
ask the waiter for (the bill)	
the waiter takes your order	
the waiter serves you	

Common expressions

Match the halves:

1. The waiter served
2. We left a big tip because
3. The waiter stood by our table,
4. We sat down and asked the waiter
5. I called the waiter over
6. My girlfriend works part-time as
7. The service was terrible and

    a. to ask for another bottle of wine.
    b. a waitress in an Italian restaurant.
    c. for a menu.
    d. ready to take our order.
    e. my wife first.
    f. the waiter was positively rude.
    g. the waitress was so friendly.

bill

Common expressions	
the bill comes to (£55)	put (the beer) on the bill
(Could we) have the bill	pay the bill
split / divide the bill	

Common expressions

Complete the sentences with the correct form of the above verbs:

1. Waiter! Could we . . . . the bill, please?
2. He left without . . . . his share of the bill. How could he do that?
3. The final bill . . . . to £126.75. There's no service charge, so let's add a £10 tip.
4. Let's . . . . the bill between the four of us. It's too much for one person to pay.
5. Waiter! I'd like another beer, please. Just . . . . it on the bill.

Note   Note these types of bill:
He ran up a huge phone bill when he was on holiday.
I always pay my electricity bills on time.
If you don't pay your gas bill, you'll be cut off.

bar

Verb + bar (the place)	Verb + bar	Adjective + bar
open / close a bar	go to the bar	a crowded bar
meet at a bar	order at the bar	a smoky bar
leave a bar	stand at the bar	a snack bar
	work behind a bar	a licensed bar

1. Verb + bar (the place)

Complete the verb phrase with the correct form of the above verbs:

1. We . . . . at Charlie's Bar every Friday evening. Come along and join us.
2. The bars . . . . early here. They stop serving drinks around ten o'clock.
3. Amy finished her drink and . . . . the bar without saying a word. It must have been something I said.

2. Verb + bar (where you order a drink)

Complete the verb phrase with the correct preposition:

1. There's no table service, sir. You can order . . . . the bar.
2. I work . . . . a bar at the weekends to help pay for my studies.
3. We stood . . . . the bar, talking about football all night.
4. It was my turn to go . . . . the bar to get a round of drinks.

3. Adjective + bar

Complete the sentences with the above adjectives:

1. The club has a . . . . bar which serves drinks from 5 till midnight.
2. I hate trying to get served in a . . . . bar.
3. . . . . bars make my eyes water.
4. There's a small . . . . bar inside the bowling alley which serves things like burgers and chips.

Note   Note these expressions:
We went off in search of a bar.
There is live entertainment in the bar at weekends.

service

Adjective + service	
the service is good / excellent / terrible / awful	the service is quick / slow

Adjective + service

Match the halves:

1. The food was good, but the service was slow.
2. The food at Dolmios was fantastic, and the service was excellent.
3. The service at the Taj Mahal is terrible and so is the food.

a. We left a large tip and we'll definitely go back there.
b. I wouldn't recommend it.
c. The first course was delicious, but we did have to wait 45 minutes for it!

menu

Verb + menu

Complete the sentences with one word. Most are verbs.

1. He . . . . the most expensive thing on the menu!
2. After I sat down, the waiter . . . . me a menu.
3. Excuse me, could we . . . . the menu, please?
4. The menu . . . . sandwiches as well as hot meals.
5. A waiter led us to our table and left us to . . . . the menu.
6. Another customer asked me if I was . . . . with the menu.
7. There was only one menu on the table so we had to . . . . it.
8. Our son is only 4. Do you do a . . . . menu?

Notes
1. Note the expression:
   Are there any vegetarian dishes on the menu?
2. We choose different *courses* from the menu:
   I'm already full and I've only eaten one course!
   I ordered a three-course meal, but I couldn't finish the sweet.
   I had soup as a starter and fish for my main course.
3. Note that a *set menu* offers limited choice for a fixed price:
   There's a set menu for dinner, but you can also choose from our à la carte menu.

"Your table's ready, sir. I'll bring you the menu."

table

Common expressions

Complete the sentences with one word from the expressions in the box:

1. Can we just turn up or do we need to . . . . a table?
2. Yes, I'm on my own – just a table for . . . . , please.
3. Do you have a . . . . table for three in about an hour?
4. Would you like to come through now? Your table's . . . .
5. If you don't have a . . . . table, I think we'll try somewhere else, thank you. My son's allergic to smoke.
6. I'm sorry, but we booked a table . . . . the window.
   > I'm sorry, sir. I think we've made a mistake. If you could wait about 5 minutes, we'll have a very nice table on the balcony. Would you like a drink on the house?

Test 9

breakfast	lunch	dinner	restaurant	waiter / waitress	bill	bar	service	menu	table

1. Identifying the key word

Choose the key word which collocates with these verbs, adjectives and nouns:

1. . . . . recommend, try out, Italian, fully-booked
2. . . . . have, pay, split
3. . . . . call, work as, friendly, rude
4. . . . . have, invite to, prepare, take out to
5. . . . . make, skip, cooked, continental
6. . . . . get, study, share, children's
7. . . . . early, three-course, packed, Sunday
8. . . . . awful, excellent, slow
9. . . . . book, wait for, free, ready
10. . . . . work behind, stand at, crowded, snack

2. The correct collocation

Choose the correct collocation:

1. I don't think it is a good idea to *avoid / skip* breakfast. It's an important meal.
2. I'm not hungry during the day and I usually just have a *light / small* lunch.
3. We'd like to *invite / offer* you to dinner on Saturday night.
4. The new Greek restaurant *serves / cooks* great food.
5. Can you *call / tell* the waiter? I'd like some more water.
6. The bill *arrives at / comes to* £67.
7. Can you give me a few minutes to *see / study* the menu, please?
8. Your table is *made / ready*. Would you like to come this way?

3. Key word quiz

Complete each sentence with the correct key word:

1. I took a packed . . . . with me when we went on the school trip to the seaside.
2. A young French . . . . took our order. He was very polite and friendly.
3. We're going out for . . . . this evening.
4. It was my turn to go to the . . . . and order the drinks.
5. When I sat down, the waiter handed me the . . . .
6. We tried to book a . . . . at Fabio's but the . . . . was fully booked.
7. I usually have cereal for . . . . , but sometimes I have a boiled egg and toast.
8. We split the . . . . between the three of us. It worked out at about £20 each.
9. The . . . . was excellent. We only waited a short while for our food to arrive.

4. Prepositions

Choose the correct preposition to complete these expressions:

1. We discussed the deal *over / with* dinner at the Sheraton Hotel.
2. The post office was closed *at / for* lunch.
3. He runs a chain *for / of* restaurants in the West End.
4. I work *behind / at* a bar in the evenings.
5. Have you got a table *by / with* the window?
6. Have they got anything spicy *in / on* the menu?

Section 10

Drink

coffee

Verb + coffee	Adjective + coffee	Noun + of + coffee
drink coffee	black / white coffee	a cup / mug of coffee
have a coffee	strong / weak coffee	a jar of coffee
make coffee	instant coffee	a sip of your coffee
pour coffee	fresh coffee	the smell of coffee
spill coffee (on the floor)	hot coffee	
	a quick coffee	

1. Verb + coffee

Complete the sentences with the correct form of the above verbs:

1. I spent much of my student life sitting around . . . . coffee.
2. The waiter . . . . me some more coffee as we waited for the bill to arrive.
3. Sorry. I've . . . . some coffee on your carpet. Have you got a wet cloth?
4. Let's . . . . a coffee before we start the shopping.
5. I'll clear the table if you . . . . the coffee. There's a jar beside the bread bin.

2. Adjective + coffee

Complete the sentences with the above adjectives:

1. I burnt my mouth on some . . . . coffee. I should have waited until it had cooled!
2. I'll make some . . . . coffee if anyone wants some more.
3. Do you take your coffee black or . . . .?
4. Do you think we've got time for a . . . . coffee before the lecture?
5. I find it difficult to get to sleep if I drink . . . . coffee in the evening.
6. We don't have any real coffee but you'll find a jar of . . . . coffee in the cupboard above the sink.

3. Noun + of + coffee

Match the halves:

1. We get through
2. I love
3. Oscar handed round
4. Any chance of
5. I took a sip of the coffee and spat it out.

a. It tasted like dishwater!
b. a whole jar of coffee every week.
c. a cup of coffee, Jill?
d. mugs of hot coffee.
e. the smell of freshly ground coffee.

Notes
1. Note these expressions:
   The neighbours invited us in for coffee.
   How do you like your coffee?
   I'm dying for a cup of coffee. (I need one now.)
2. Note these kinds of coffee:
   Instant coffee consists of coffee granules. Real coffee is made with coffee beans.
   You grind coffee beans to make filter coffee or an expresso.
   Decaffeinated coffee is coffee with no caffeine in it.

"Coffee is so last century, my dear! It's all lattes, expressos and cappuccinos now!"

tea

Verb + tea	Adjective + tea	Common expressions
drink tea	strong / weak tea	a cup / mug of tea
have tea	hot tea	a pot of tea
make tea	sweet tea	a drop of tea
serve tea	iced tea	have milk in (your) tea
bring (you) tea		

1. Verb + tea

Complete the sentences with the correct form of the above verbs:

1. When the programme ended, I put the kettle on to . . . . some tea.
2. Waiters in white uniform . . . . tea and cakes to the guests at the garden party.
3. I'm getting tired. Let's stop at the next service station and . . . . some tea.
4. My husband . . . . me a cup of tea in bed this morning.
5. We sat down and . . . . our tea in silence.

2. Adjective + tea

Complete the sentences with the above adjectives:

1. We tried to cool down by drinking lots of . . . . tea.
2. She makes the tea too . . . . You can hardly taste it!
3. Yuk! This tea's too . . . . How many spoonfuls of sugar did you put in it?
4. I blew on the . . . . tea to cool it down.

3. Common expressions

Match the halves:

1. We'd like scones and a pot
2. I usually start the day
3. Would you like a drop of tea?
4. I like milk in my tea,

a. with a cup of tea.
b. I've just made some.
c. but there's none in the fridge.
d. of tea for two, please.

"There's nothing like a nice cup of tea!"

Notes

1. Note this way of saying you really need some tea:
   I could murder a cup of tea right now!
2. Note how we describe drinking tea:
   He gulped his tea down and rushed back to work. (drank quickly)
   She sipped her tea slowly.
   He slurped his tea. (made a noise as he drank)
3. You don't need to say 'cup of' when ordering tea:
   Two teas, a doughnut, and a piece of chocolate cake, please.
4. You can also get *green tea, herbal tea, China tea, Indian tea,* etc.
5. You can buy tea in *teabags* or *loose:*
   Don't forget to get a packet of tea bags. We've none left.
   Could you get some loose tea – maybe a packet of Assam and a packet of Earl Grey.
   I hate real tea – all those tea leaves! I much prefer tea made with a teabag.

beer

Verb + beer	Adjective + beer	Noun + of + beer
drink beer	a cool / cold beer	a bottle of beer
have a beer	bottled / draught beer	a can of beer
brew beer	low-alcohol beer	a six-pack of beer
order a beer	the beer is flat	a pint of beer

1. Verb + beer

*Complete the sentences with the correct
form of the above verbs:*

1. The Czech Republic is famous
   for the fantastic beers it . . . .
2. The waiter came to the table when you
   were at the toilet, so we . . . .
   you another beer. Is that OK?
3. . . . . a beer, Greg. This German
   lager is very good. Try it.
4. I don't . . . . beer, so I'll have a
   whisky if you've got one.

"From six-pack to beer belly!"

2. Adjective + beer

Complete the sentences with the above adjectives:

1. I'll have a . . . . beer as I'm driving. If they don't have any, just get me a soft drink.
2. There's nothing like a . . . . beer to satisfy your thirst after a hard game of tennis.
3. My beer was . . . . – there was no fizz in it. So I took it back to the bar.
4. They don't have any . . . . beer – they only have bottles. Do you still want one?

3. Noun + of + beer

Match the halves:

1. I was so thirsty,
2. I had a plate of pasta,
3. After the party the streets were
4. I bought a six-pack of beer

a. washed down with a bottle of beer.
b. littered with empty beer cans.
c. to take to the barbecue.
d. I downed two pints of beer in 5 minutes.

Note

1. In 1d in exercise 3 'down' means to drink – usually quickly. Note this other way of saying this:
   He knocked back his beer and left the bar.
2. A beer belly describes a large stomach:
   His beer belly hangs over his belt. It's a pretty ugly sight.
3. A 'six-pack' can refer to a pack of 6 bottles or cans of beer or it can refer to the muscles on a man's
   body.
4. Alcoholic drinks like vodka, whisky and rum are called *spirits*. Note these expressions:
   I poured myself a glass of whisky.
   I'd like a large / double whisky, please.
   I always drink whisky neat / straight. (with nothing in it)
5. In the UK you order beer at a bar in the following ways:
   A bottle of Grolsch, please.
   A pint of Stella, please.
   A pint of bitter, please.

wine

Verb + wine	Adjective + wine	Common expressions
drink wine	a white / red wine	a bottle of wine
pour wine	a sweet / dry wine	a glass of wine
serve wine	an expensive / a cheap wine	a case of wine
store wine	a good / fine wine	the effect of wine
spill wine (on the table)	a sparkling wine	

"Do have one of these little fishy things – and help yourself to the wine!"

1. Verb + wine

Complete the sentences with the correct form of the above verbs:

1. I can't . . . . any wine tonight. I'm taking antibiotics.
2. The red wine I . . . . on my best shirt has left a stain on it.
3. It's best to . . . . wine in a cool dry place.
4. White wine is best . . . . chilled.
5. I held up my glass and the waiter . . . . some wine for me.

2. Adjective + wine

Complete the sentences with the correct form of the above adjectives:

1. I don't like sweet wines. I prefer very . . . . wines.
2. It might be a . . . . wine, but I don't think it's champagne.
3. Australia now produces some of the . . . . wines in the world.
4. I generally have . . . . wine with fish and red with a meat dish.
5. It's a very . . . . wine, but it tastes all right. What do you think?

3. Common expressions

Match the halves:

1. We stayed in last night and shared a pizza and
2. My doctor says I should limit myself to
3. I liked the wine so much that
4. I don't really like the taste of wine.
5. My father believes in

a. two glasses of wine a day.
b. a bottle of wine.
c. I much prefer beer.
d. the beneficial effects of red wine.
e. I bought a whole case of it.

Note   Note these wine + noun expressions:
Can I see the wine list, please?
I don't have a wine cellar but I keep one or two bottles in a wine rack in the dining room.
He's a real wine connoisseur / buff. (knows a lot about wines)

bottle

Verb + bottle	Adjective + bottle	Common expressions
open a bottle	a plastic bottle	pull a cork out of a bottle
shake a bottle	the bottle is full / half full /	unscrew the top off a bottle
recycle bottles	empty	put the cap back on a bottle
drink a bottle of (beer)		the label on a bottle
pass a bottle to (you)		

1. Verb + bottle

Complete the sentences with the correct form of the above adjectives or verbs:

1. During the meal, we . . . . four large bottles of mineral water between the three of us.
2. I can't . . . . this bottle. Could you have a try?
3. I think about the environment a lot. For example, I . . . . all my bottles and cans.
4. Alena poured herself a glass of wine, then . . . . the bottle to me.
5. I think that . . . . bottles are much safer to use than traditional glass ones.
6. You're meant to . . . . the bottle before you open it, so that the contents mix together.
7. The bottle was nearly . . . . when I put it in the fridge last night. Now it's almost
. . . . ! So who's been drinking my milk?

2. Common expressions

Complete the sentences with the correct preposition:

1. Can you unscrew the top . . . . this bottle for me?
2. There's no label . . . . the bottle, so I'm not sure what kind of wine it is.
3. I couldn't pull the cork out . . . . the wine bottle. It was stuck fast.
4. Make sure you put the cap . . . . on the bottle of shampoo when you've finished.

Note   Note these expressions:
When we got to our hotel room, there was a complimentary bottle of champagne waiting for us! (a free bottle)
It's one of those parties where you bring your own bottle. (BYOB!)

glass

Verb + glass	Common expressions
fill up (your) glass	a cracked glass
raise (your) glasses	an empty glass
knock over a glass	fill a glass to the brim
hold out your glass	raise your glass to your lips
a glass smashes	a wine glass

1. Verb + glass

Complete the sentences with the correct form of the above verbs:

1. I accidentally . . . . over a glass of red wine as I was passing their table.
2. The glass fell out of my hand and . . . . on the floor.
3. I . . . . out my glass for some more wine as the waiter was passing.
4. What a party! As soon as your glass was empty, a waiter . . . . it up!
5. Let's all . . . . our glasses and wish George and Mary a happy anniversary!

2. Common expressions

Match the halves:

1. Some of these glasses are cracked.
2. Please don't fill my glass to the brim.
3. You can't drink beer
4. Will you collect
5. She raised the glass

a. I don't want to spill wine on my dress.
b. out of a wine glass! I'll get you a beer mug!
c. to her lips and took a sip of wine.
d. the empty glasses from the tables, please?
e. We'll need to replace them.

cup

Verb + cup	Common expressions
pick up your cup	a clean / dirty cup
hold your cup	a full cup
prefer a cup	half a cup
fill a cup (up) with (tea)	a chipped cup
knock over a cup	a plastic cup
hand (you) a cup	

an egg cup a cup of tea a cup of coffee pouring milk into a cup

1. Verb + cup

Complete the sentences with the correct form of the above verbs:

1. The cup was so hot I couldn't . . . . it in my hand.
2. The waiter came across and . . . . my cup with more coffee.
3. Do you . . . . a cup to a mug?
4. The baby . . . . over a full cup of tea at the dinner table. What a mess!
5. The nurse . . . . me a cup of water to help me swallow the medicine.
6. He . . . . up his cup and saucer and sipped his tea.

2. Common expressions

Complete the sentences with one word:

1. Can I just have . . . . a cup, please? I'm not very thirsty.
2. The cup was . . . . so we had to throw it out.
3. The problem with . . . . cups is that they aren't very good for hot drinks.
4. Will you put all the . . . . cups in the dishwasher, please?

Note   Note that we use 'cup' to mean the contents of the cup – tea. coffee, etc:
Would you like another cup?
I've already had three cups!
He drained his cup and then poured himself another. (He drank it quickly.)

Test 10

coffee	tea	beer	wine	bottle	glass	cup

1. Identifying the key word

Choose the key word which collocates with these verbs, adjectives and nouns:

1. .... open, shake, half full, plastic
2. .... drink, dry, sweet, white
3. .... drink, fresh, instant, mug
4. .... pick up, hold, chipped, clean
5. .... have, make, sweet, pot
6. .... fill up, knock over, smash, cracked
7. .... drink, brew, cold, flat

2. The correct collocation

Choose the correct collocation:

1. Would you *do / make* some coffee while I wash up the dishes?
2. Don't leave the teabag in the cup for very long. I only drink *light / weak* tea.
3. I'm sorry, we don't have *draught / tap* beer. We only have bottles.
4. Could you *unscrew / turn* the top off this bottle for me, please?
5. I knocked *down / over* Peter's wine glass as I reached for the salt.
6. I'd like some *icy / iced* tea, please.
7. I don't drink *strong / thick* coffee late at night. It keeps me awake!

3. Key word quiz

Complete each sentence with the correct key word:

1. Is it a sweet or dry ....?
2. The government is trying to encourage us to recycle our empty ....
3. I don't like instant .... I much prefer filter or expresso.
4. In my opinion, the best .... in the world is brewed in the Czech Republic.
5. I raised the .... to my lips and took a sip of wine. It was quite nice.
6. I don't drink .... or coffee. I only drink mineral water.
7. When we finished having tea, I put all the dirty .... in the dishwasher.

4. Noun phrases

Choose the correct noun to complete these noun phrases:

1. I'll just go out and buy another .... of coffee. This one's nearly empty.
2. We'd like a coffee and a .... of tea for two, please.
3. He bought a six- .... of beer from the supermarket.
4. There are usually 12 bottles in a .... of wine.
5. How much is a half .... of beer?

5. Expressions

Complete these expressions with one word:

1. Have we got time for a .... coffee before the film starts?
2. I couldn't read the .... on the bottle.
3. The glass was .... , so I had to throw it away.
4. I like .... wines like champagne and cava.
5. I'd rather have a .... of tea than a cup.

Section 11

Shopping and food 1

shop

Verb + shop	Types of shop	Common expressions
the shop opens / closes (at 9)	a coffee shop	buy (it) in a shop
the shop sells (newspapers)	a pet shop	take (it) back to the shop
work in a shop	a shoe shop	steal (a tie) from a shop
go (down) to the shops	a souvenir shop	wander around the shops
run a shop	a toy shop	be available in the shops
break into a shop	a small / corner shop	
leave the shop	a charity shop	

1. Verb + shop

Complete the sentences with the correct form of the above verbs:

1. My neighbour is the manager of a shoe shop in London. He's been . . . . it for 5 years.
2. WH Smiths is a really good shop. It . . . . a wide range of magazines.
3. We'll need to . . . . to the shops today – we've got no food in the house.
4. The shop . . . . at 8am, but it's closed for lunch between 12.30 and 1.30.
5. I always check my change before I . . . . the shop.
6. My girlfriend . . . . in a shoe shop in the Gyle shopping centre.
7. Thieves . . . . into the shop last night and stole a number of DVD recorders.

2. Types of shop

Match the halves:

1. We went to three pet shops before we	a. it was full of cheap gifts.
2. Today it's difficult for small shops to	b. There's a Starbucks on nearly every corner!
3. I got him a computer game	c. from charity shops. They're cheaper there.
4. Like many souvenir shops,	d. found a cat that we both liked.
5. I get most of my clothes	e. from the local toy shop.
6. Coffee shops are opening up everywhere.	f. compete against the big supermarkets.

3. Common expressions

Complete the expressions with the correct preposition:

1. The security guard caught him trying to steal two pairs of trousers . . . . the shop.
2. My wife bought the most expensive dress . . . . the shop!
3. If there's something wrong with the clock, take it back . . . . the shop.
4. I love wandering . . . . the shops at the weekend.
5. There are many different types of MP3 player available . . . . the shops.

Notes

1. Note these expressions:
   The shop was out of milk. (It had none left.)
   My flat is handy for the shops. (It's near the shops.)
   The shop is open 24 hours a day.
   The shops are always busier at the weekend.

2. Note these expressions with 'shopping':
   Shopping is one of my favourite pastimes.
   We're going shopping after work. Do you want to come along?
   You can do your shopping from home using the internet.
   Late-night shopping is becoming very popular.
   I've got to do some last-minute shopping for Christmas presents.
   Have you tried internet shopping?

supermarket

Common expressions

shop at the supermarket
open a new supermarket
stack shelves at the supermarket

stop at the supermarket
need something from the supermarket

Common expressions

Complete the sentences with the correct form of the above verbs:

1. Do you . . . . anything from the supermarket? I'm just going down there.
2. I usually . . . . at the local supermarket.
3. There are plans to . . . . another new supermarket in our area!
4. Can we . . . . at the supermarket on the way home?
5. I've got a job . . . . shelves at a supermarket.

Notes

1. In a supermarket you put things into a *trolley* or a *basket*.
2. You pay at the *checkout*.

"She's about this size."

customer

Common expressions

serve customers
attract new customers
a regular customer

treat customers (well / badly)
deal with a difficult customer
a satisfied / dissatisfied customer

Common expressions

Match the halves:

1. I'd call the manager. He's used to dealing
2. Supermarkets are cutting prices
3. Mrs Wilson is one of our regular customers.
4. There are always hundreds of satisfied customers
5. You must always be polite when
6. You'll never keep your customers

a. for every dissatisfied one.
b. if you treat them badly.
c. you are serving the customers.
d. with difficult customers.
e. to attract new customers.
f. She's been coming here for years.

meat

Verb + meat	Adjective + meat
eat meat	fresh meat
cook meat	frozen meat
fry meat	raw meat
slice meat	red / white meat
chop meat into (pieces)	tender / tough meat
meat goes off	undercooked meat

1. Verb + meat

Complete the sentences with the correct form of the above verbs:

1. We . . . . the meat in the oven for 2 hours. That's what the recipe said. But it's ruined!
2. I don't . . . . meat now. I've been a vegetarian for two years.
3. . . . . the meat in a little oil, before adding the vegetables and spices.
4. This meat smells as if it has . . . . off. I think I'll need to throw it out.
5. Could you . . . . the meat thinly, and put it on the plates?
6. . . . . the meat into small cubes with a sharp knife, then fry gently for about 5 minutes.

2. Adjective + meat

Match the halves:

1. This meat's quite tough.	a. It was almost raw.
2. You should always allow frozen meat	b. red meat these days.
3. The meat was hardly cooked at all.	c. I can't cut it!
4. Eating undercooked meat is	d. to defrost overnight.
5. Cook the meat slowly	e. a common cause of food poisoning.
6. For health reasons, I'm eating less and less	f. until it is tender.

Note

Note these expressions:
The meat was cooked to perfection. It was delicious.
I always trim the fat off meat before cooking it.
I had a large slice of roast beef in a sandwich for lunch today.

chicken

Common expressions		
kill a chicken	roast a chicken	chicken wings, legs, thighs, breasts
cut a chicken (into pieces)	chicken soup	rub a chicken with (oil / garlic)

Common expressions

Match the halves:

1. My mother always gives us chicken soup	a. roast a large chicken.
2. Cut the chicken into	b. before putting it in the oven.
3. We usually buy chicken thighs.	c. eat it. What about you?
4. Rub the chicken with garlic	d. pieces and mix them with the sauce.
5. I could never kill a chicken, then	e. They're cheaper than chicken breasts.
6. It only takes about 2 hours to	f. when we're ill.

fish

Verb + fish	Common expressions
catch fish	raw fish
cook / grill / fry fish	oily fish
(the kitchen) stinks of fish	fish and chips

Common expressions

Match the halves:

1. My son caught two fish this morning.
2. Grill the fish for 3 minutes on each side,
3. I've only ever eaten raw fish once.
4. I'll have to stop eating fish and chips.
5. I eat oily fish such as mackerel once a week,
6. The rubbish bin stinks of fish.

a. I'm putting on too much weight!
b. because it's good for my health.
c. We're having them for dinner tonight.
d. Can you wash it out, please?
e. or fry it for a few minutes in a little oil.
f. It was in a sushi bar in Tokyo.

oil

Verb + oil	
heat the oil	fry (the fish) in oil
pour oil over (the meat)	add oil to (the salad)

Verb + oil

Complete the sentences with the correct form of the above verbs:

1. . . . . the strips of meat in a little sunflower oil until they turn brown.
2. . . . . some oil in a large pan for a few minutes, then add the garlic and onion.
3. . . . . a little olive oil and fresh herbs to the pasta, then mix thoroughly before serving.
4. . . . . some oil over the chicken, then place it in the oven.

egg

Common expressions		
boil / fry / scramble / poach an egg	break an egg	a chicken lays eggs
a hard-boiled / soft-boiled egg	a fried egg	scrambled eggs
a dozen eggs		

Common expressions

Match the halves:

1. How long does it take to
2. I fried myself an egg and a couple of
3. I'd like to know how many eggs
4. We had scrambled eggs
5. Can you get me half a dozen eggs,
6. Do you like the yolk
7. Would you like your egg

a. hard-boiled or soft-boiled?
b. a chicken lays in a week.
c. on toast for breakfast.
d. rashers of bacon.
e. in your fried eggs hard or runny?
f. when you're at the supermarket?
g. boil an egg?

milk

Verb + milk	Common expressions
heat milk	low fat / semi-skimmed milk
use up the milk	warm milk
pour milk (into a jug, cup)	a bottle / carton of milk
take milk in (your tea)	a pint / litre of milk
milk comes from (cows)	be allergic to milk
	the milk smells off

1. Verb + milk

Complete the sentences with the correct form of the above verbs:

1. I . . . . the milk from the carton into a jug, and put it on the breakfast table.
2. Do you . . . . milk in your tea?
3. Believe it or not, I was 8 before I learned that milk . . . . from cows!
4. Can you . . . . the milk for the baby's bottle, please?
5. Someone's . . . . up all the milk! What am I going to put on my cereal?

2. Common expressions

Match the halves:

1. My son is allergic to cows' milk,
2. This milk smells off.
3. Milk came in bottles when I was a boy.
4. We've recently switched over to low fat milk.
5. I usually have a cup of warm milk before bed.

a. It's much better for you.
b. so I have to buy goat's milk.
c. I find it helps me to sleep.
d. I'll open a new carton just to be safe.
e. It comes in cartons now.

cheese

Common expressions		
cut cheese	grate cheese	hard / soft cheese
grated cheese	mouldy cheese	low-fat cheese
a chunk of cheese		

Common expressions

Match the halves:

1. Low-fat cheeses are becoming very popular
2. I bought bread and a large chunk of cheese
3. We found a piece of mouldy cheese
4. I take soft cheeses to work because
5. Grate the cheese, then
6. Could you cut me

a. a piece of cheese, please?
b. sprinkle it over the mashed potatoes.
c. they are easy to spread on bread.
d. at the bottom of the fridge.
e. to have for lunch.
f. with people who are trying to lose weight.

Note   Note the expression:
She can't eat dairy products such as milk and cheese. She's allergic to them.

vegetables

Verb + vegetables	Adjective + vegetables
grow vegetables	fresh vegetables
cook / boil / steam vegetables	frozen vegetables
overcook the vegetables	green vegetables
store vegetables	organically-grown vegetables

1. Verb + vegetables

Complete the sentences with the correct form of the above verbs:

1. I usually . . . . vegetables rather than boil them. They have more flavour that way.
2. We . . . . all our own vegetables in our garden.
3. You need to . . . . vegetables in a cool dry place.
4. The meat was fine, but the vegetables were . . . . and tasteless.

2. Adjective + vegetables

Match the halves:

1. All these vegetables are home-grown.
2. I prefer to buy organically-grown vegetables.
3. Fresh vegetables taste much better than
4. There are lots of vitamins in

a. green vegetables.
b. frozen vegetables.
c. I think they're safer to eat.
d. They're fresh from the garden.

fruit

Verb + fruit	Adjective + fruit
wash fruit	fresh fruit
peel fruit	dried fruit
pick fruit	citrus fruit
fruit rots	ripe / unripe fruit

1. Verb + fruit

Complete the sentences with the correct form of the above verbs:

1. Some fruit, like oranges and bananas, has to be . . . . before you can eat it.
2. Farmers spray fruit with a lot of chemicals these days, so it's a good idea to . . . . all fruit before you eat it.
3. We had to throw the oranges out. They had started to . . . .
4. I had a temporary job . . . . fruit in Greece during the summer holidays.

2. Adjective + fruit

Match the halves:

1. You get a lot of vitamin C from
2. I try to eat at least three pieces
3. I carried a packet of dried fruit and
4. Leave the fruit until it's ripe.

a. It'll taste better if you wait until it's ready.
b. nuts to give me energy on the walk.
c. of fresh fruit every day.
d. citrus fruits like oranges and limes.

Test 11

supermarket   shop   customer   meat   chicken   fish   oil   egg   milk   cheese   vegetables   fruit

1. Identifying the key word

Choose the key word which collocates with these verbs, adjectives and nouns:

1. . . . .   catch, fry, oily, raw
2. . . . .   kill, roast, wings, thighs
3. . . . .   open, shop at, stop at
4. . . . .   attract, serve, regular, satisfied
5. . . . .   grated, low-fat, mouldy, chunk
6. . . . .   heat, low fat, carton, litre
7. . . . .   add, heat, pour
8. . . . .   peel, pick, dried, fresh
9. . . . .   boil, fried, hard-boiled, scrambled
10. . . . .   chop, fry, slice, raw
11. . . . .   work in, pet, shoe, toy
12. . . . .   grow, fresh, frozen, green

2. The correct collocation

Choose the correct collocation:

1. I think this milk smells *off* / *out*.
2. Mrs Orwell is one of our *regular* / *usual* customers.
3. The meat was cooked to perfection. It was very *soft* / *tender*.
4. *Cook* / *Heat* the oil gently, then add the vegetables and fry for a few minutes.
5. Do you *add* / *take* milk in your coffee?
6. We get lots of *fresh* / *new* vegetables from our garden.

3. Key word quiz

Complete each sentence with the correct key word:

1. I got a job stacking shelves at the local . . . .
2. We've had frozen burgers every day this week! We haven't had fresh . . . . for ages.
3. One of my favourite meals is . . . . and chips.
4. Make sure you peel the . . . . before you eat it.
5. Fry the meat in a little . . . .
6. The supermarket has reduced all prices by 10% to attract new . . . .
7. I'd like a litre of . . . . and a kilo of cheese.
8. Can you tell me how long it takes to boil an . . . . ?
9. I grated some . . . . over the vegetables.
10. I'd rather shop at my local corner . . . . than go to a supermarket.

4. Prepositions

Choose the correct preposition to complete these expressions:

1. The new games console will be available *at* / *in* the shops from Monday.
2. Could you chop the meat *for* / *into* pieces?
3. My son is allergic *to* / *with* cows' milk.
4. I love wandering *around* / *to* the shops at the weekend.

Section 12

Food 2

bread

Common expressions	Adjective + bread	Noun + of + bread
make bread	fresh bread	a loaf of bread
cut / slice bread	brown / white bread	a slice of bread
spread bread with (butter)	rye / wholemeal bread	a (large) chunk of bread
bread goes stale	sliced bread	the smell of freshly baked bread

1. Verb and adjective collocations

Match the halves:

1. Could you spread some butter
2. My grandmother has always made
3. Bread goes stale quickly
4. The baker sells white, brown,
5. I always buy sliced bread because
6. Fresh bread is delivered daily

   a. to our local store.
   b. if you don't cover it.
   c. on the bread, please?
   d. I usually make a mess if I cut it myself.
   e. wholemeal and rye bread.
   f. her own bread.

2. Noun + of + bread

Complete these sentences with the above nouns:

1. There was a delicious . . . . of freshly baked bread coming from the kitchen.
2. Put a couple of . . . . of bread in the toaster, would you?
3. They serve hot bowls of soup with huge . . . . of bread in the school canteen. It's better for you than burgers and chips!
4. My mother took a large . . . . of wholemeal bread from the bread bin and sliced it thickly.

sandwich

Verb + sandwich			
have a sandwich	make a sandwich	order a sandwich	serve a sandwich

Verb + sandwich

Complete the sentences with the correct form of the above verbs:

1. When the waiter came to our table, I . . . . a ham sandwich and a cup of coffee.
2. I normally just . . . . a sandwich for lunch. I'm never that hungry at that time of day.
3. We only do main meals in the restaurant, but we . . . . sandwiches and other snacks in the bar.
4. Why don't we buy a loaf of bread and some cheese, and . . . . some sandwiches to take on the journey?

Notes
  1. Note these verb collocations:
     I'll fix you a sandwich. (make you one)
     I had no time for lunch so I grabbed a sandwich on the way to the station.
  2. Note these common expressions:
     What do you want in your sandwich?
     Would you like a cheese sandwich?

cake and biscuit

Expressions with cake	Verb + cake	Expressions with biscuit
a birthday cake	bake / make a cake	pass the biscuits
a wedding cake	eat a cake	plain biscuit
a chocolate cake	cut a cake	chocolate biscuit
a home-made cake	try a cake	a packet of biscuits
a recipe for a cake		cheese and biscuits
a slice / piece of cake		

fairy cakes *a cake*

a cake stand   *slices of cake*   *a piece of cake*   *a birthday cake*   *a wedding cake*

1. Verb + cake

Complete the sentences with the correct form of the above verbs:

1. Who's . . . . all the cake? I was hoping to have some with my coffee!
2. I'm . . . . a special cake for Andrew's 21st birthday.
3. Would you like to . . . . one of my mother's tea cakes?
4. Get your camera! The bride and groom are about to . . . . the wedding cake.

2. Expressions with cake

Complete the sentences with the above nouns:

1. I managed to blow out all 30 candles on my . . . . cake.
2. Would you like another . . . . of cake?
3. She says these cakes are . . . . , but I think she got them from the supermarket!
4. This carrot cake is fantastic. You must give me the . . . . for it.
5. My diet doesn't allow me to eat . . . . cake. It has too many calories in it.

3. Expressions with biscuit

Match the halves:

1. Annette passed round	a. or a piece of fruit?
2. I've got to cut out	b. if you don't mind.
3. Would you prefer cheese and biscuits	c. pass the biscuits, please?
4. I'll just have a plain biscuit	d. chocolate biscuits from my diet.
5. Do you think you could	e. a packet of biscuits during the coffee break.

Notes

1. Note the verb + preposition in the following:
   She divided the cake (equally) among the children.
   She divided the cake into ten (equal) slices.
2. Note these ways of saying the cake was good:
   Her cakes are delicious. / Her cakes are (simply) out of this world.
3. The idiom 'It was a piece of cake' means that something was very easy to do:
   The exam was a piece of cake. I finished half an hour before the end.

pasta

Verb + pasta	Common expressions
boil pasta	a (large) helping of pasta
cook pasta	a bowl of pasta
drain the pasta	a plate of pasta
eat pasta	the pasta sticks to the pot

1. Verb + pasta

Complete the sentences with the correct form of the above verbs:

1. Pasta is the easiest thing in the world to . . . . ! My mother usually over-cooks it and it's horrible!
2. I think you only need to . . . . fresh pasta for about 5 minutes before it's ready to eat.
3. I always . . . . a lot of pasta when I'm in Italy.
4. When the pasta is cooked, ... it over the sink, then add the sauce and serve. What could be simpler!

2. Common expressions

Match the halves:

1. She gave me a huge helping of pasta,
2. The waiter placed a huge bowl of pasta
3. There wasn't enough water in the pot,
4. I gave him a large plate of pasta

a. so some of the pasta stuck to the bottom.
b. and he finished it in minutes!
c. but I couldn't finish it.
d. in the middle of the table.

rice

Common expressions			
grow rice	eat rice	wash rice	served with rice
boiled / fried rice	a bowl of rice	a grain of rice	a diet of rice

Common expressions

Match the halves:

1. The refugees are living on
2. She gave me a large bowl of rice and
3. Make sure you wash the rice thoroughly
4. I think curry is best served with
5. It is a fact that rice is eaten
6. Unfortunately, the country can't grow
7. The bag of rice had a hole in it, so

a. enough rice to feed its people.
b. by more than half of the world's population.
c. boiled rice or fried rice.
d. before cooking it.
e. a pair of chopsticks.
f. grains of rice fell all over the kitchen floor.
g. a simple diet of rice and fish.

Notes
1. There are lots of different kinds of rice:
   brown rice *basmati* *white rice* *long-grain rice* *short-grain rice*
2. *Rice pudding* is rice boiled with milk and sugar.
3. A *rice dish* is a dish made with rice:
   Risotto is a kind of rice dish.

potatoes

Verb + potatoes			
grow potatoes	boil potatoes	peel the potatoes	slice the potatoes

Verb + potatoes

Complete the sentences with the correct form of the above verbs:

1. Potatoes need to .... for about 15-20 minutes before they're ready.
2. My mother was standing at the sink, ... potatoes for dinner.
3. Could you .... the potatoes thickly and we'll have chips tonight with the chicken.
4. We .... our own potatoes in our garden. We plant them in the spring and dig them up around August.

Note   Note the different ways of cooking and serving potatoes:
Boiled / mashed / roast potatoes
A baked potato

peeling potatoes   *making chips*   *mashing potatoes*   *a plate of chips*

chips

Common expressions			
fish and chips	a bag of chips	a portion of chips	greasy chips

Common expressions

Match the halves:

1. My meal came with a huge portion of chips.
2. Two bags of chips please. And can you
3. The chips were terrible.
4. I'd like fish

a. and chips, please.
b. They were awful – all soft and greasy!
c. put some salt and vinegar on them, please.
d. There was too much for one person.

Note   Note that thinly-cut potatoes, usually sold in packets, are called *potato crisps* in the UK and *potato chips* in the US. They are either *flavoured* or *plain*:
All I had for lunch was a packet of cheese and onion crisps.
I love bacon-flavoured crisps.

chocolate

Common expressions

like chocolate	be addicted to chocolate
chocolate melts	break off a piece / square of chocolate
milk / plain chocolate	a box of chocolates
dark / white chocolate	a bar of chocolate

Common expressions

Complete the sentences with the correct form of a word from the above expressions:

1. Unfortunately, the chocolate had . . . .
   in my pocket. What a mess it had made!
2. I prefer milk chocolate to . . . .
   chocolate – it's much sweeter. What about you?
3. He . . . . off a piece of chocolate, and gave
   it to the child to try to get it to stop crying.
4. I think I'm . . . . to chocolate. I eat at least
   two . . . . a day!
   > Well, I . . . . chocolate, but I can take it
   or leave it.
5. My sister gave us some chocolates on our
   wedding anniversary, and we ate the whole
   . . . . between us in a night.

Note Note these expressions with 'sweets':
Don't eat a lot of sweets – they're bad for your teeth.
As a child I spent most of my pocket money on sweets.

"We ate the whole box in one evening!"

sugar

Verb + sugar

contain sugar
have / take sugar in (tea)
put sugar on something
sprinkle sugar on / over (the fruit)

Common expressions

a teaspoon / spoonful of sugar
a sachet of sugar
a sugar cube
a (high / low) sugar content
your intake of sugar
take (a sweetener) in place of sugar

1. Verb + sugar

Complete the sentences with the correct form of the above verbs:

1. Do you . . . . sugar in your tea?
2. It's pure fruit juice. It . . . . no added sugar so it's OK for diabetics.
3. When you take the cakes out of the oven, ... a little granulated sugar over them.
4. Jason, there's no need to . . . . sugar on your cereal. It's sweet enough already!

2. Common expressions:

Match the halves:

1. If you're serious about losing weight,	a. in place of sugar.
2. Most canned soft drinks have a	b. No wonder she has such bad teeth.
3. I tore open the sachet of sugar and it	c. high sugar content.
4. She puts five spoonfuls of sugar in her tea!	d. spilled all over the table.
5. There's some sugar cubes	e. in the bowl on the table.
6. Try adding fruit to your breakfast cereal	f. reduce your intake of sugar.

Notes

1. Note this expression:
   I like two sugars in my coffee. (two spoonfuls)
2. A sugar *cube* is sometimes called a sugar *lump*.
3. If something has *a high sugar content*, we sometimes say that it is *high in sugar*:
   Most junk food is high in sugar and salt.
4. You sometimes read on labels that something is *sugar-free* or has *no added sugar*.
   Is this juice sugar-free?
   Natural orange juice with no added sugar.

salt

Verb + salt	Common expressions
pass the salt	a pinch of salt
cut down on salt	a (level) teaspoon of salt
add salt to (the soup)	high / low in salt
sprinkle salt on / over (your chips)	your salt intake
	salt and pepper

1. Verb + salt

Complete the sentences with the correct form of the above verbs:

1. Norma, could you . . . . the salt, please?
2. I think if we . . . . some salt to the soup, it will taste better.
3. I usually . . . . a little salt on my food to give it flavour, especially boiled vegetables.
4. I have high blood pressure and the doctor has advised me to . . . . down on the amount of salt I'm eating.

2. Common expressions

Match the halves:

1. Don't add too much salt.	a. with salt and pepper.
2. You should avoid foods like crisps	b. our salt intake.
3. A level teaspoon of salt	c. which are high in salt.
4. Most of us should reduce	d. should be enough.
5. Season the soup	e. Just a pinch will do.

Notes

1. Note these expressions:
   Salt helps to bring out the flavour in food.
   A lot of tinned food is high in salt.
   Hey! Go easy on the salt. Too much salt is bad for your health.
2. The sea is made up of *salt water*. Lakes are made up of *fresh water*.
   I don't like swimming in the sea. I hate getting salt water in my eyes.

Test 12

| bread | sandwich | cake | biscuit | pasta | rice | potatoes | chips | chocolate | sugar | salt |

1. Identifying the key word

Choose the key word which collocates with these verbs, adjectives and nouns:

1. . . . .   grow, boil, peel, slice
2. . . . .   make, slice, fresh, brown
3. . . . .   add, cut down on, pass, pinch of
4. . . . .   plain, chocolate, packet
5. . . . .   bake, cut, birthday, recipe
6. . . . .   melt, dark, milk, bar
7. . . . .   grow, boiled, fried, grain of
8. . . . .   have, make, order, ham, cheese
9. . . . .   contain, sprinkle, cube, sachet
10. . . . .   boil, cook, drain, eat
11. . . . .   greasy, bag, portion

2. The correct collocation

Choose the correct collocation:

1. Could you *cover / spread* some butter on the toast, please?
2. Let's *do / make* some sandwiches for lunch.
3. Honestly! I *baked / cooked* the cake myself.
4. Mike, could you *peel / skin* the potatoes and slice them for chips?
5. I don't like milk chocolate. I'd rather have *dark / strong* chocolate.

3. Key word quiz

Complete each sentence with the correct key word:

1. I ordered a cup of coffee and a ham . . . .
2. I love fish and . . . .
3. No dessert for me, thanks. I'll just have some . . . . and cheese.
4. I try to eat wholemeal . . . . I think it's much better for your health.
5. I much prefer plain boiled . . . . to fried . . . .
6. I failed to blow out all the candles on my birthday . . . . I must be getting old!
7. Sprinkle a little . . . . over the potatoes before you serve them.
8. Drain the . . . . , then serve it with a little olive oil.

4. Noun phrases

Choose the correct noun to complete these noun phrases:

1. I bought a large unsliced . . . . of bread from the supermarket.
2. You must give me the . . . . for your orange and chocolate cake.
3. Would you like another . . . . of cake?
4. What a greedy thing! He ate the whole . . . . of biscuits himself.
5. I had a large . . . . of pasta for lunch today.
6. There were some . . . . of rice at the bottom of the kitchen cupboard.
7. They serve huge . . . . of chips at Divernos.
8. I was so hungry I ate a whole . . . . of milk chocolate.
9. Can you bring me a couple of . . . . of brown sugar from the counter? I forgot.
10. I only put a . . . . of salt on my food. Too much salt is bad for you.

Section 13

Your body

body

Common expressions

your body aches
exercise your body
move your body (to music)
a dead body

your body shakes
be self-conscious about your body
have a great / amazing body
your body is run-down

Common expressions

Match the halves:

1. I had the flu last week and
2. People moved their bodies
3. Swimming is an excellent way of
4. When I got out of the car after the accident,
5. She has an amazing body
6. You're more likely to get sick
7. The first time I ever saw a dead body was
8. I'm very self-conscious about my body.

a. I think my legs are too thin.
b. exercising your body.
c. my whole body was shaking.
d. in time to the music.
e. when your body is run-down.
f. at my grandmother's funeral.
g. for a woman of 60.
h. my body was aching all over.

"I think I've got a great body!"

muscle

Common expressions

build up / develop your muscles
massage (tense) muscles
(a bath) soothes tired muscles

relax / tense your muscles
pull a muscle
muscles feel stiff

Common expressions

Complete these sentences with the correct form of the above verbs:

1. Try not to . . . . the muscles in your stomach so much. Breathe out slowly and try to relax them.
2. I use weights in the gym to . . . . up my muscles.
3. Our best player won't be able to play on Saturday because he's . . . . a muscle.
4. After a hard day at work, I get my wife to . . . . the tense muscles in my back.
5. My leg muscles usually . . . . stiff for days after I've run a marathon.
6. After the football match, I had a long, hot bath to . . . . my tired and aching leg muscles.

Note   Note this expression:
How can the guards at the palace gates stand for hours without moving a muscle?

skin

> **Common expressions**
>
> have fair / dark skin   your skin is itchy
> hard / soft skin   scrape the skin off (your knees)
> your skin peels

Common expressions

Match the halves:

1. If you have very fair skin,
2. My skin is so itchy,
3. I crashed my motorbike
4. I keep my skin soft
5. I find his dark skin and black eyes
6. I got badly sunburnt on holiday and

a. now the skin is beginning to peel off my arms.
b. and scraped all the skin off my knees.
c. I can't stop scratching myself.
d. very attractive.
e. by using lots of hand cream.
f. you shouldn't sit in the hot sun for very long.

Note   A 'scar' is a mark left on the skin when a cut heals:
He had a big scar across his cheek.
The cut is quite deep, and it will probably leave a scar.

stomach

> **Verb + stomach**   **Common expressions**
>
> hold your stomach   a full stomach
> lie on your stomach   an upset stomach
> something upsets your stomach   a strong stomach
> your stomach rumbles   pick up a stomach bug
>   hit someone in the stomach

1. Verb + stomach

Complete the sentences with the correct form of the above verbs:

1. My stomach was . . . . during the lesson. I should have had some breakfast before going to school. It was very embarrassing.
2. I don't eat hot spices like chillies. They . . . . my stomach, and give me wind!
3. Geraldine was . . . . on her stomach, watching television, when I got home.
4. My dad was . . . . his stomach because it was very painful. But it was nothing serious – just a touch of indigestion.

2. Common expressions

Match the halves:

1. You should never swim on a full stomach.
2. I missed college yesterday because of
3. The doctor told me not to take these pills on
4. The film is full of blood and guts! You'll need
5. I picked up a nasty stomach bug
6. I don't know why he hit me

a. in the stomach.
b. an empty stomach. I have to eat first.
c. an upset stomach.
d. while I was on holiday.
e. a strong stomach to watch it.
f. You might get cramp.

waist and back

Expressions with waist	Expressions with back
strip to the waist	hurt your back
put your arms round (his) waist	lie on your back
wrap (a towel) round your waist	pat someone on the back
(your hair) reaches to your waist	a sore / bad back

1. Expressions with waist

Complete the sentences with the correct form of the above verbs:

1. While we were dancing, he . . . . his arms round my waist and kissed me on the cheek.
2. I got out of the bath and . . . . a towel round my waist to see who was at the door.
3. Our teacher's got incredibly long hair. It . . . . down to her waist!
4. At boarding school we had to . . . . to the waist and wash ourselves in cold bathrooms.

2. Expressions with back

Match the halves:

1. I love getting my back rubbed.	a. lifting some furniture.
2. My back is sore after all that	b. with a bad back.
3. We lay on our backs in the sun	c. heavy work in the garden!
4. I hurt my back while I was	d. It's so relaxing.
5. He's been off work for over a month now	e. gazing up at the sky.

arm

Verb + arm	Adjective + arm	Common expressions
fold your arms	a broken arm	put his arms round her
break an arm	a stiff arm	hold (a baby) in your arms
your arm aches	long / short arms	carry (a file) under your arm
		stick a needle into (your) arm

1. Verb and adjective collocations

Complete the sentences with the correct form of the above adjectives or verbs:

1. My right arm is so . . . . after playing tennis yesterday. I can hardly bend it at all today!
2. Mark is perfect as goalkeeper. He's tall, with really big hands and . . . . arms.
3. My grandmother fell awkwardly as she got off the bus, and . . . . her arm in two places.
4. My arms are . . . . after carrying these heavy shopping bags from the supermarket.
5. How can he write with a . . . . arm?
6. The prisoner sat down, ... his arms across his chest and refused to speak.

2. Common expressions

Complete these sentences with the correct preposition:

1. Mr Morris came into the room, carrying a newspaper . . . . his arm.
2. When I met Angela at the airport, she put her arms . . . . me and gave me a big hug.
3. Your mother was holding a large cat . . . . her arms when she opened the door.
4. I tried not to cry, but it really hurt when the nurse stuck the needle . . . . my arm.

Note   If you welcome someone *with open arms*, you are very pleased to see them.

wrist

Verb + wrist			
break your wrist	sprain your wrist	cut your wrists	hold your wrist

"I'm not cutting my wrists! I'm filing my nails!"

Verb + wrist

Complete the sentences with the correct form of the above verbs:

1. Liz wasn't trying to kill herself. I think . . . . her wrists was a cry for help.
2. I . . . . my wrist in my exercise class last week. At first I thought I'd broken it!
3. The nurse . . . . my wrist in order to check my pulse.
4. My father fell and . . . . his wrist. It was in plaster for ages. It's still not right!

leg

Verb + leg	**Common expressions**
break your leg	fat / thin legs
shave your legs	tired legs
rub your leg	stiff legs
lose your leg (in a war / an accident)	balance on one leg
(doctors) amputate your leg	stretch your legs out

1. Verb + leg

Complete the sentences with the correct form of the above verbs:

1. I . . . . my leg skiing, but I can walk quite well with crutches.
2. My best friend has an artificial leg. He . . . . his left leg in a car accident 5 years ago.
3. It's common for women to . . . . their legs regularly. Some footballers are now doing it!
4. Why are you . . . . your leg?
   > I bumped into the corner of the table. It's really sore!
5. Doctors had to . . . . the farmer's legs below the knee after he stood on a landmine.

2. Common expressions

Match the halves:

1. I don't think I look good in short skirts.	a. rest your weary legs.
2. At the end of the long flight from Tokyo	b. balance on one leg?
3. There wasn't enough room in the car for me to	c. My legs are too fat.
4. You must be exhausted. Here, sit down and	d. stretch my legs out.
5. Can you shut your eyes and	e. my legs were very stiff.

finger

Common expressions

cut your finger	snap your fingers
tap your fingers (on the table)	point your finger at someone
have / wear a ring on your finger	lick (the chocolate) off your fingers
hold (a match) between your finger and thumb	

Common expressions

Match the halves:

1. I accidentally cut my finger while
2. In the UK, it's not the custom to snap your fingers
3. Tommy! Stop tapping your fingers on the desk.
4. In the UK, it's rude
5. I finished the cake,
6. James was holding a 50p coin
7. I love jewellery.

a. then licked the cream off my fingers.
b. to point your finger at someone.
c. I have a ring on every finger!
d. between his finger and thumb.
e. I was chopping some onions.
f. to attract a waiter's attention.
g. It's driving me up the wall!

Note   To 'keep your fingers crossed' is to hope for good luck:
We'll just have to keep our fingers crossed that it doesn't rain.

nail and toe

Verb + nail	Expressions with toe
grow your nails	touch your toes
cut your nails	stand on your toes
paint your nails	step on someone's toes
break a nail	be covered in (mud) from head to toe
bite your nails	

1. Verb + nail

Complete the sentences with the correct form of the above verbs:

1. Damn! I've . . . . one of my nails again.
2. I use a pair of nail clippers to . . . . my nails. I never use scissors.
3. Anastasia's not ready yet. She's still . . . . her nails!
4. How do you expect your nails to . . . . if you . . . . them all the time!

2. Expressions with toe

Complete the sentences with the correct form of the above verbs:

1. I had to . . . . on my toes to see out of the church window.
2. Can you bend over and . . . . your toes? I can't.
3. Sorry! I didn't mean to . . . . on your toes.
4. After the rugby match, most of the boys were . . . . in mud from head to toe.

Notes   1. Note this expression:
You've still got some dirt under your nails. Get back upstairs and wash your hands properly.

2. If you *file your nails*, you use a *nail file* or *emery board* to make them smooth after you have cut them.

knee

Common expressions

bend your knees	hurt your knee
scrape / graze your knees	get down on your hands and knees
have / need an operation on your knee	(the water) came right up to your knees

Common expressions

Complete the sentences with the correct form of the above verbs:

1. I . . . . my knee quite badly while playing football. The doctors think I may . . . . an operation on it.
2. Always remember to . . . . your knees when lifting heavy objects or you'll hurt your back.
3. We had to wade across the stream and the water . . . . right up to our knees!
4. I . . . . down on my hands and knees and looked under the bed for my other sock.
5. Jamie tripped over a stone which was lying on the pavement and . . . . his knees. His mother had to put a couple of plasters on them when he got home.

foot

Verb + foot	**Adjective + foot**	**Common expressions**
wash your feet	your bare feet	my feet are killing me
wipe your feet	smelly feet	be unsteady on your feet
lift your feet	dirty feet	be on your feet all day
stand on someone's foot	your feet are freezing	go / travel on foot

1. Verb + foot

Complete the sentences with the correct form of the above verbs:

1. Make sure you . . . . your feet before you enter the swimming pool.
2. Ali! Don't shuffle along like that! . . . . your feet properly when you're walking.
3. Ouch! You're . . . . on my foot! Why don't you watch where you're going!
4. Please . . . . your feet on the mat before you come into the house.

2. Adjective + foot

Complete the sentences with the correct form of the above adjectives:

1. Elena! Don't walk around in your . . . . feet. Put some shoes on!
2. After walking through the snow in my trainers, my feet were absolutely . . . .
4. Whatever you do, don't let Costas take his shoes off. He's got really . . . . feet!
5. Katerina. Get your feet off the sofa – they're . . . . !

3. Common expressions:

Match the halves:

1. My feet are killing me!
2. I've been in bed with the flu all week and
3. I've been on my feet all day and
4. You could save money by going to work

a. I just want to sit down and rest.
b. on foot instead of taking the bus.
c. I'm still unsteady on my feet.
d. I've been shopping all day.

Test 13

body muscle skin stomach waist back arm wrist leg finger nail toe knee foot

1. Identifying the key word

Choose the key word which collocates with these verbs and adjectives:

1.	. . . .	fair, dark, itchy, soft
2.	. . . .	break, bite, grow, paint
3.	. . . .	lie on, rumble, full, upset
4.	. . . .	break, fold, stiff, long
5.	. . . .	bend, hurt, graze, scrape
6.	. . . .	cut, point, snap, tap
7.	. . . .	hurt, lie on, bad, sore
8.	. . . .	wash, wipe, bare, smelly
9.	. . . .	massage, pull, tense, stiff
10.	. . . .	strip to, put (a towel) round
11.	. . . .	ache, exercise, dead, run-down
12.	. . . .	break, stretch, thin, tired
13.	. . . .	stand on, step on, touch
14.	. . . .	break, cut, hold, sprain

2. The correct collocation

Choose the correct collocation:

1. When I had the flu my body was *hurting / aching* all over.
2. I *hurt / pulled* a muscle in my leg while I was playing tennis and had to stop.
3. She ate something that *hurt / upset* her stomach.
4. I *hurt / upset* my back lifting some heavy boxes.

3. Key word quiz

Complete each sentence with the correct key word:

1. He broke his left . . . . playing football. He's now on crutches.
2. I fell off my bike and scraped all the . . . . off my knees and elbows.
3. I don't know how he can walk across the hot sand in his bare . . . .
4. He sat down and folded his . . . . across his chest.
5. I missed breakfast and my . . . . was rumbling all through the meeting.
6. Can you touch your . . . . ? I can only do it if I bend my . . . .
7. He snapped his . . . . to attract the waiter's attention.
8. He's been off work for months with a bad . . . .
9. After work, I got my wife to massage the tense . . . . in my neck.
10. Believe it or not, his hair reaches down to his . . . .

4. Prepositions

Choose the correct preposition to complete these expressions:

1. Don't point your finger *at / to* me!
2. He was carrying a newspaper *in / under* his arm.
3. The teacher patted me *in / on* the back and said 'Well done!'
4. I wrapped a towel *round / on* my waist.
5. I don't know why he hit me *in / on* the stomach.
6. He apologised for stepping *on / over* my toes.

Section 14

Head and shoulders

hair

Verb + hair	Adjective + hair
brush / comb your hair	long / short hair
wash your hair	wet / dry hair
cut your hair	fair / grey / dark hair
get your hair cut	straight / curly hair
lose your hair	
dye your hair	

1. Verb + hair

Complete these expressions with the correct form of the above verbs:

1. How often do you . . . . your hair? I usually do mine when I have a shower.
2. Your hair's a mess! Make sure you . . . . it before you go into the meeting!
3. Does your sister . . . . her hair, or is that her natural colour?
4. Where do you get your hair . . . . ?
   > I don't! My wife . . . . it to save money.
5. Serge started . . . . his hair in his twenties. He's now completely bald.

2. Adjective + hair

Complete the sentences with the above adjectives:

1. I've got straight hair, but my brother's hair is naturally . . . .
2. My dad's in his forties now, and he's starting to get a few . . . . hairs.
3. I usually wear a cap in the shower to keep my hair . . . .
4. Gunnar is a typical Swede with . . . . hair and blue eyes.
5. Don't go out with . . . . hair. You can borrow my hairdryer.
6. Vera looks better with . . . . hair. You could hardly see her face when her hair was so long!

Notes
1. Hair which is very fair can be described as *blond / blonde*.
   My girlfriend's got long blonde hair and blue eyes.
2. Note that men get their hair *cut*. Women have their hair *done*.
   Have you seen Derek? He's just had his hair cut. It's really short. It doesn't suit him.
   Liz is having her hair done this afternoon. She's getting married tomorrow.

beard and moustache

Verb + beard / moustache	
have a beard / moustache	grow a beard / moustache
shave off your beard / moustache	trim your beard / moustache

Verb + beard / moustache

Complete these expressions with the correct form of the above verbs:

1. I hardly recognised you with a beard! How long have you . . . . one?
2. We weren't allowed to . . . . beards at high school.
3. I usually . . . . my beard about once a week to keep it tidy.
4. My girlfriend wants me to . . . . off my moustache. She thinks it makes me look old.

face

Verb + face	**Common expressions**
wash your face	put a name to a face
never forget a face	have a smile on your face
splash your face with water	go red in the face
wipe your face (with a towel)	tell (him) straight to (his) face
Adjective + face	your face is covered in / with (mud)
a familiar face	(sweat) is running down your face
an honest face	
a long face	
a straight face	

"Why the long face?"   "She had a smile on her face."   "I can't put a name to her face."   "I never forget a face!"

1. Verb + face

Complete these expressions with the correct form of the above verbs:

1. Our headteacher is good at remembering former pupils. She never . . . . a face.
2. The sweat was running down my face during the match. I had to keep . . . . it.
3. I always . . . . my face and shave first thing in the morning.
4. I was feeling sleepy, so I . . . . my face with cold water to waken myself up.

2. Adjective + face

Match the halves:

1. His face is familiar,
2. He has an honest face,
3. Why the long face?
4. I can never play jokes on people because

a. Has someone upset you?
b. I can't keep a straight face!
c. so I think we can trust him.
d. but I can't remember where I've met him.

3. Common expressions

Complete the expressions with the correct preposition:

1. I told him straight . . . . his face that I thought he was wrong.
2. He had a big smile . . . . his face when he came out of the manager's office.
3. The driver's face was covered . . . . blood.
4. I'm sure I know him, but I can't put a name . . . . the face!
5. I was so embarrassed when the girl I liked talked to me. I just went red . . . . the face.
6. Eva was clearly upset when she came into the room. Tears were running . . . . her face.

Note   Note how we use the expression 'a look on (your) face' to describe feeling and emotion:
I'll never forget the look of disappointment on her face when she heard she had failed her exam.
You should have seen the look on his face when I told him I'd won the lottery!
I could tell by the look on his face that he wasn't happy.

mouth

Verb + mouth	Common expressions
open / close your mouth	a (funny, horrible) taste in your mouth
burn your mouth	put something in your mouth
wipe your mouth (with a tissue)	talk with your mouth full
	(the food) makes your mouth water

1. Verb + mouth

Complete these expressions with the correct form of the above verbs:

1. I wish he'd . . . . his mouth when he's eating! It's not a pretty sight!
2. The dentist asked me to . . . . my mouth wide.
3. At the end of the meal I . . . . my mouth with the napkin.
4. The tea . . . . my mouth. I should have waited until it had cooled down a little!

2. Common expressions

Match the halves:

1. Don't talk	a. in my mouth.
2. The medicine left a horrible taste	b. swallowed it whole.
3. He put a strawberry into his mouth and	c. made my mouth water.
4. The wonderful smell of baking	d. with your mouth full!

Notes 1. If you are very nervous, your mouth *goes dry*.
In the middle of my speech, my mouth went dry. It was good I had a glass of water!
2. The *mouth of a river* is where it enters the sea.

tooth

Verb + tooth / teeth	Adjective + tooth / teeth
brush your teeth	healthy teeth
lose your teeth	bad teeth
have a tooth taken out	false teeth
break a tooth	a missing tooth

1. Verb + tooth / teeth

Complete these expressions with the correct form of the above verbs:

1 I fell off my bike last week and . . . . three of my teeth.
2. You should get into the habit of . . . . your teeth after meals.
3. I've still got all my front teeth, but I've . . . . most of my back ones.
4. I'm going to the dentist this afternoon to have two teeth . . . . out.

2. Adjective + tooth / teeth

Match the halves:

1. Both my parents have false teeth.	a. Some of them are actually black!
2. Healthy gums	b. got broken when he was playing football.
3. My son's front teeth	c. I hope I never need to have any!
4. I wish she'd do something about her bad teeth.	d. are as important as healthy teeth.

tongue, lips, kiss, smile

tongue	lips	kiss	smile
bite your tongue	lick your lips	give (him) a kiss	a friendly smile
burn your tongue	lift ... to your lips	your first kiss	a lovely smile
stick your tongue out	dry lips	a big kiss	have a smile on (his)
(at someone)		a goodnight kiss	face

1. Verb collocations

Complete these sentences with the correct form of the above verbs:

1. I . . . . my tongue on the soup. It was far too hot.
2. His interview must have gone well. When he came out, he . . . . a big smile on his face.
3. I . . . . my lips at the thought of all the lovely food we would have at the party.
4. A little boy . . . . his tongue out at me on the bus today. What a cheek!
5. She . . . . the glass to her lips and slowly sipped her wine.
6. I accidentally . . . . my tongue while I was eating! It's still quite sore.

2. Adjective collocations

Complete these sentences with the above adjectives:

1. When I arrived at the airport, my wife ran up to me and gave me a . . . . kiss.
2. The hotel receptionist greeted me with a . . . . smile.
3. My mother always gave us a . . . . kiss before she turned out the lights.
4. My lips are really . . . . and sore. I'll need to put some cream on them.
5. Linda is a very warm person, and she has such a . . . . smile.
6. I don't think anybody ever forgets their . . . . kiss. Do you remember yours?

"I'll just put on some lipstick."   "I got a fish bone stuck in my throat."   "He'll never forget his first kiss!"

throat

Common expressions		
your throat hurts	(food) sticks in your throat	a sore throat
grab (him) by the throat	cut (your) throat	

Common expressions

Match the halves:

1. I got a fish bone stuck
2. If your throat hurts,
3. All the dead sheep
4. Because of my sore throat,
5. Someone grabbed me by the throat and

a. tried to strangle me.
b. in my throat and had to go to hospital.
c. I found it difficult to swallow food.
d. had had their throats cut.
e. try sucking one of these throat sweets.

ear

Common expressions

put your hands over your ears	whisper in (her) ear
have a sore ear	get your ears pierced
your ears stick out	

Common expressions

Complete these expressions with the correct form of the above verbs:

1. Tom . . . . a sore ear again. I'll need to get some ear drops from the chemists.
2. She doesn't like her ears because they . . . . out. She keeps her hair long to hide them.
3. If you want to start wearing earrings, you'll need to get your ears . . . . first.
4. Henry leaned over to Fiona at the meeting and . . . . something in her ear.
5. I . . . . my hands over my ears, so that I couldn't hear the baby crying.

Note

Note these expressions:
The music at the concert was very loud. My ears are still ringing! (full of a ringing noise)
I'm a little deaf in one ear.

"Her ears stick out."   "He's picking his nose again!"   "He's blowing his nose."   "I put my hands over my ears."

nose

Verb + nose

blow your nose	wipe your nose
hold your nose	pick your nose
break your nose	your nose runs
your nose bleeds	your nose is blocked

Verb + nose

Complete these expressions with the correct form of the above verbs:

1. The smell was so bad that I had to . . . . my nose and leave the room.
2. Alice took out her handkerchief and . . . . her nose loudly.
3. Frank . . . . his nose while he was talking to me. What a disgusting habit!
4. How can I stop my nose . . . .?
   > Put your head back and hold it between two fingers. That's what I always do.
5. My nose is often . . . . and I have to breathe through my mouth.
6. I've got a cold and my nose is . . . . Has anyone got a tissue so that I can wipe it?
7. One of our sons . . . . his nose playing rugby. It happened to me when I was at school.
8. Have you got a tissue? The baby's nose needs . . . .

neck

Common expressions

break your neck

have a stiff neck

wear (a necklace) round your neck

a pain in the neck

Common expressions

Match the halves:

1. Chris fell from his horse and broke his neck.
2. Steve can be a real pain in the neck.
3. I woke up with a stiff neck this morning.
4. Mary was wearing

a. a silver chain round her neck.
b. It must have been the way I was lying.
c. He's now paralysed from the neck down.
d. He never does what he says he will.

Notes

1. Note that in number 2 *a pain in the neck* is someone who is very annoying or irritating.
   I wish she wouldn't tell lies. She can be a real pain in the neck.

2. An annoying situation can also be *a pain in the neck.*
   I wish they would turn that music down. I'm trying to work. It's just a pain in the neck!

shoulder

Verb + shoulder

have (broad) shoulders

shrug your shoulders

massage your shoulders

dislocate your shoulder

look over your shoulder

Common expressions

put your arm round someone's shoulders

carry your bag over your shoulder

(your bag) slips off your shoulder

tap someone on the shoulder

lift someone onto your shoulders

lean your head on someone's shoulders

1. Verb + shoulder

Complete the sentences with the correct form of the above verbs:

1. I . . . . my shoulder while I was playing rugby and had to be taken to hospital.
2. You'll recognise Joe easily. He's really tall and . . . . very broad shoulders.
3. My neck and shoulders are really tense. Will you . . . . them for me?
4. I kept . . . . over my shoulder to see if anyone was following me.
5. We complained about our hotel room, but the manager just . . . . his shoulders!

2. Common expressions

Complete the sentences with the correct preposition:

1. When she started to cry, I put my arm . . . . her shoulders.
2. If you tighten the straps of your backpack, it won't slip . . . . your shoulders.
3. She leaned her head . . . . my shoulder and fell asleep within minutes.
4. He carried his schoolbag . . . . his shoulder.
5. I tapped the girl . . . . the shoulder and asked her if she was in the queue.
6. I lifted my little brother . . . . my shoulders so that he could get a better view.

Note

A bag which a woman carries over one shoulder is called *a shoulder bag.*
She was carrying a beautiful green leather shoulder bag. I think it was Gucci. It must have cost a fortune.

Test 14

hair	face	mouth	tooth	tongue	lip	beard / moustache
kiss	smile	throat	ear	nose	neck	shoulder

1. Identifying the key word

Choose the key word which collocates with these verbs, adjectives and nouns:

1. . . . .   wash, forget, familiar, honest
2. . . . .   blow, hold, run, wipe
3. . . . .   brush, wash, lose, curly
4. . . . .   cut, grab by, sore
5. . . . .   brush, bad, false, healthy
6. . . . .   open, close, burn, wipe
7. . . . .   have, grow, shave off, trim
8. . . . .   lick, dry
9. . . . .   cover, stick out, sore, big
10. . . . .   have, big, friendly, lovely
11. . . . .   dislocate, look over, shrug
12. . . . .   break, stiff, a pain in
13. . . . .   bite, burn, stick out
14. . . . .   give, first, big, goodnight

2. The correct collocation

Choose the correct collocation:

1. You won't believe it, but Ann's *coloured / dyed* her hair orange!
2. My brother had two teeth taken *out / away* at the dentist's yesterday.
3. I used a napkin to *clean / wipe* my mouth at the end of the meal.
4. I woke up this morning with *an aching / a sore* throat.
5. Have you got a tissue? I need to *clean / blow* my nose.
6. He just *raised / shrugged* his shoulders and said he didn't know where the money was.

3. Key word quiz

Complete each sentence with the correct key word:

1. I splashed my . . . . with water in order to wake myself up.
2. I hope I never have to get false . . . .
3. I've got a really stiff . . . . this morning. I'm finding it difficult to turn my head.
4. I'm going to shave off my . . . . My wife says she wants to see my face again!
5. I got a fish bone stuck in my . . . . and had to go to hospital.
6. My . . . . were so dry that I had to put some cream on them.
7. You'll recognise her quite easily. She's got long, curly . . . .
8. I accidentally bit my . . . . while I was eating an apple. It's really sore now.

4. Prepositions

Choose the correct preposition to complete these expressions:

1. The medicine left a horrible taste *in / on* my mouth.
2. He wears a gold chain *on / round* his neck.
3. He had a big smile *on / over* his face.
4. She was carrying a large bag *on / over* her shoulder when she arrived.
5. There's no need to shout *in / to* my ear. I can hear you quite clearly.

Section 15

Clothes

trousers

Verb + trousers	Common expressions
wear trousers	a pair of trousers
pull on your trousers	long / short trousers
iron your trousers	tight / loose trousers
take a size (14) in trousers	your trouser pocket
try on trousers	your trouser leg

1. Verb + trousers

Complete the sentences with the correct form of the above verbs:

1. Have you got an iron I could borrow? I need to . . . . these trousers.
2. . . . . on these trousers and see if they fit you.
3. I used to . . . . a size 10 in trousers when I was 18, but I'm afraid I'm now a size 18!
4. I . . . . on my trousers, and got up to answer the door.
5. I remember that you were . . . . blue trousers and a striped shirt when I first met you.

2. Common expressions:

Match the halves:

1. I need a new	a. to primary school.
2. You'll find some loose change	b. up my trouser legs.
3. Zak's trousers are too short.	c. I'll have to get a bigger size.
4. These trousers are too tight for me now.	d. They don't even reach his shoes.
5. We had to wear short trousers	e. pair of trousers for work.
6. The wind was blowing	f. in my back trouser pocket.

shirt

Common expressions	
wear a shirt	a plain / striped / checked shirt
a short-sleeved / long-sleeved shirt	a clean / dirty shirt
a cotton shirt	a T-shirt
your shirt collar	your shirt sleeves

Common expressions

Match the halves:

1. He was wearing jeans	a. but you do have to iron them!
2. Do you know your collar's dirty?	b. comfortable in the summer.
3. I prefer cotton shirts,	c. and a T-shirt with 'Feed the World' on it.
4. Although I work in an office,	d. and started washing the dishes.
5. I find short-sleeved shirts much more	e. I think it's time you put on a clean shirt.
6. I rolled up my shirt sleeves	f. I don't need to wear a shirt and tie.

Notes
1. *An open-necked shirt* means you do not have the top button done up.
2. You *button up* your shirt and *unbutton it.*
3. Note this expression:
   One of my shirt buttons is missing.

tie

Common expressions

wear a tie	put on a tie	loosen your tie
tie your tie	a plain tie	a black tie
your old school tie		

Common expressions

Complete the sentences with the correct form of words from the above expressions:

1. I was very hot, so I . . . . my tie and undid the top button of my shirt.
2. You can't eat in the hotel dining room unless you're . . . . a tie.
3. Do you have a . . . . tie I could borrow? I have to go to a funeral tomorrow.
4. My old . . . . tie had orange and red stripes on it. What was yours like?
5. I can't . . . . a tie on properly by myself! I have to get my mother to help me.
6. Can you . . . . a tie? I never seem to be able to do it properly!
7. I prefer . . . . ties to patterned ones.

sweater

Verb + sweater	**Common expressions**
wear a sweater	a thick sweater
put on a sweater	a woollen sweater
knit a sweater	have your sweater on inside out
wash a sweater	pull your sweater over your head
a sweater shrinks	

1. Verb + sweater

Complete the sentences with the correct form of the above verbs:

1. This is a cashmere sweater and needs to be . . . . by hand.
2. I'm . . . . your father a sweater for Christmas, but don't tell him!
3. At the party, Laura was . . . . a sweater with a golf logo on it.
4. My sweater has . . . . a little. Maybe I shouldn't have put it in the tumble drier!
5. I'd . . . . on a sweater. I think it's going to get colder later.

2. Common expressions

Match the halves:

1. I hate woollen sweaters.
2. Donald! You've got your sweater on
3. I can't pull this sweater over my head.
4. She was wearing a thick sweater

a. I think it's a couple of sizes too small!
b. made of Merino wool.
c. They make my arms itch!
d. inside out again!

Notes
1. Other words for *sweater* are *pullover* and *jumper*.
2. A sweater which fastens at the front with buttons is called a *cardigan*.
3. A sweater with a very high neck is called *a polo neck sweater*.
4. Other kinds of sweater are:
   a hand-knitted sweater   a woollen / cashmere sweater   a heavy / light sweater

dress

Verb + dress	Common expressions
try on a dress	a long / short dress
wear a dress	an old / a new dress
make a dress	a cotton dress
the dress fits you	look fantastic / sensational in a dress
the dress fastens (at the back)	(your hat) goes with / matches your dress

1. Verb + dress

Complete the sentences with the correct form of the above verbs:

1. That's a very nice dress you're . . . . Is it silk?
2. If the dress doesn't . . . . me, can I bring it back and get my money back?
3. This dress . . . . at the back. Can you zip me up, please?
4. There weren't any changing rooms in the shop for me to . . . . on the dress.
5. My wife . . . . her own wedding dress. It saved us a lot of money!

2. Common expressions

Match the halves:

1. You can't wear those green shoes!
2. Beyonce looked absolutely sensational in
3. Sheila wore a long white dress
4. I'm looking for a blue handbag
5. Why don't you put on your new dress?
6. On holiday in India, I wore

a. I haven't seen it on you yet.
b. which reached all the way to the ground.
c. short cotton dresses and sandals all the time.
d. the dress she wore to the MTV awards.
e. They don't go with your dress.
f. to match this dress.

coat

Verb + coat	Adjective + coat
put your coat on	a fur coat
wear a coat	a long coat
take your coat off	a winter coat
hang your coat up	

1. Verb + coat

Complete the sentences with the correct form of the above verbs:

1. Let's . . . . our coats on and go out for a walk.
2. When I got home from the party, I discovered I was . . . . the wrong coat!
3. Jan! Don't throw your coat on the floor. . . . . it up in the hall.
4. . . . . your coat off and make yourself at home. I'll go and make some tea.

2. Adjective + coat

Complete the sentences with the above adjectives:

1. It was snowing heavily outside, so I put on my . . . . coat.
2. . . . . coats have gone out of fashion. People don't like the idea of killing animals.
3. During our chemistry lessons we have to wear . . . . white coats.

hat

Verb + hat

wear a hat   put on / take off a hat   try on a hat

hold on to your hat   (the wind) blows your hat off

a beret   *a cap*   *a cocktail hat (a fancy hat)*   *a sun hat*

Verb + hat

Complete the sentences with the correct form of the above verbs:

1. I . . . . on lots of different hats, but I couldn't find one that I liked.
2. I hate . . . . hats because they usually make my head too hot.
3. For my own safety, I had to . . . . on a hard hat when I visited the building site.
4. During the storm, I had to . . . . on to my hat in case it blew away.
5. Make sure that you . . . . your hat off when you go into the mosque.

uniform

Common expressions

wear a uniform   change into / out of your uniform

be in uniform   school uniform

army uniform   a nurse's uniform

Common expressions

Match the halves:

1. I change out of my school uniform
2. I think Mark looks really smart
3. Do you have to wear a uniform
4. General Rivers wasn't in uniform.
5. Your sister looks completely different
6. School uniforms are no longer

a. in his army uniform.
b. in her nurse's uniform.
c. compulsory in many British schools.
d. if you work at Pizza Hut?
e. That's why I didn't recognise him at first.
f. into jeans and a T-shirt when I get home.

Notes
1. A soldier can be *in uniform* or *out of uniform*.
2. Other kinds of uniform are *naval uniform, prison uniform, a pilot's uniform*.
3. One of the most common adjectives used with *uniform* is *smart*.

scarf and gloves

Expressions with scarf	Expressions with gloves
wear / tie a scarf round your neck	wear gloves
a football / school scarf	put on / take off gloves
a long scarf	rubber / leather / woollen gloves
	a pair of gloves

    rubber gloves   *gloves*   *a long woolly scarf*   *a silk scarf*   *a head scarf*

Common expressions

Match the halves:

1. Can you help me? I'm having trouble	a. in order to tie my shoe laces.
2. I put on my coat and wound	b. when I do the washing up.
3. Why don't you throw those old gloves away	c. wear football scarves to school.
4. I had to take off my gloves	d. putting on these gloves.
5. We're not allowed to	e. a long scarf around my neck.
6. I always wear rubber gloves	f. and buy a new pair!

sock

Verb + sock	Common expressions
wear socks	a pair of socks
change your socks	woollen socks
put on your socks	ankle / knee-length socks
	sports socks
	a hole in your sock

1. Verb + sock

Complete the sentences with the correct form of the above verbs:

1. Give me a minute to . . . . my shoes and socks on, and I'll come with you.
2. When the weather is this hot, I don't . . . . socks.
3. What a smell! I wonder when he last . . . . his socks.

2. Common expressions:

Match the halves:

1. Why not give Uncle George	a. a hole in your sock?
2. I need to buy some new sport socks	b. look silly!
3. Do you know you've got	c. warm woollen socks for the winter.
4. My gran always knits me	d. a pair of socks for Christmas?
5. I think ankle socks and trainers	e. before the tennis match this weekend.

shoe

tennis shoe	brogue	sandal	flat shoe
wedge shoe	high-heeled shoe	evening shoe	court shoe

1. Verb + shoe

Complete the sentences with the correct form of the above verbs:

1. Can I . . . . on these shoes in a size 44, please?
2. The shoes I'm . . . . are far too tight for me. They're hurting my feet.
3. I . . . . my school shoes until I could almost see my face in them!
4. We . . . . off our shoes and socks, and walked barefoot along the beach.

2. Common expressions

Match the halves:

1. I've just bought a new
2. Abby was wearing brown leather shoes
3. I've got some chewing gum
4. We'll be doing a lot of walking,
5. I usually wear
6. I've got a hole in my running shoes,

a. stuck to the sole of my shoe.
b. so I'll need to get a new pair.
c. with pointed toes to the party.
d. flat shoes without heels to work.
e. so bring some walking shoes with you.
f. pair of tennis shoes in the sales.

Notes

1. Note these expressions:
   What size shoe do you take?
   These shoes are a good fit.
2. A *boot* is a stronger kind of shoe which normally covers your ankles:
   I'll need a new pair of climbing boots if we're going to the Alps.
3. Note these expressions with 'lace':
   Be careful. Your laces are undone.
   I bent down to tie my shoelace.
   He untied his shoelaces and kicked off his shoes.

Test 15

trousers	shirt	tie	sweater	dress	coat	hat	uniform	scarf	gloves	sock	shoe

1. Identifying the key word

Choose the key word which collocates with these verbs, adjectives and nouns:

1. ....   take off, polish, leather, pair
2. ....   wear, put on, rubber, pair
3. ....   wear, knit, thick, woollen
4. ....   wear, long, football, school
5. ....   be in, change out of, school, nurse's
6. ....   change, knee-length, woollen, hole
7. ....   wear, striped, sleeve, collar
8. ....   wear, hold onto, take off, blow off
9. ....   make, try on, long, cotton
10. ....   put on, loosen, plain
11. ....   hang up, take off, fur, long
12. ....   pull on, long, short, pair

2. The correct collocation

Choose the correct collocation:

1. I prefer shirts with long *arms / sleeves*.
2. Your hat *fits / matches* your coat. You look great!
3. The dress *closes / fastens* at the back.
4. These shoes don't *fit / match* me. I'll need a bigger size.

3. Key word quiz

Complete each sentence with the correct key word:

1. I wear short-sleeved .... to work in the summer months.
2. I'd never wear a fur ....
3. It was so hot in the room that I had to take off my jacket and loosen my ....
4. A strong gust of wind blew my .... off my head.
5. His feet really smell. I wish he'd change his .... more often.
6. I'm afraid your .... has shrunk a little. I washed it in hot water by accident.
7. Andrew, don't forget to polish your .... for school tomorrow.
8. I'm putting on weight around the waist. I'll need to buy a new pair of ....
9. He was wearing a football .... round his neck when he left.
10. She was wearing a long, cotton .... which fastened at the back.
11. Could you do the washing up, John? There's a pair of rubber .... by the sink.
12. I always change out of my school .... as soon as I get home.

4. Prepositions

Choose the correct preposition to complete these expressions:

1. I got out of bed and pulled *on / in* my trousers.
2. I'd like to try *on / with* this dress. Where are the changing rooms?
3. I couldn't pull the sweater *on / over* my head. It was too small.
4. Your new shoes go *on / with* your dress. They're a perfect match.
5. I've got a hole *in / on* my new socks already!

Section 16

Personal items

pocket

Common expressions

search in your pocket for (your key)
empty your pockets
an inside pocket

go through your pockets
a back pocket
a hole in my pocket

Common expressions

Complete the sentences with one of the above words:

1. I .... in my pockets for some change for the bus, but I didn't have enough for the fare.
2. The teacher asked the whole class to .... all their pockets to find out who had stolen Javier's pen.
3. The key must have fallen through a .... in my trouser pocket.
4. Make sure you .... through the pockets of your jeans before you put them into the washing machine.
5. It's not a good idea to carry your passport in the .... pocket of your jeans!
6. I always keep my wallet in the .... pocket of my jacket.

Notes
1. You can talk about your *jacket pocket* or your *coat pocket*.
2. The pocket in your trousers is your *trouser pocket* – not your *trousers pocket*.

belt, button, zip

Expressions with zip

do up your zip
your zip is undone / open
the zip is broken

Expressions with belt

wear a belt
tighten / loosen your belt
unbuckle your belt
a money belt
a leather belt

Verb + belt / button / zip

do up / undo / fasten / unfasten

Expressions with button

sew a button on (your shirt)
a button came off
a button is missing
the top or bottom button

Common expressions

Complete these sentences with one of the above words:

1. The zip at the back of your dress is slightly undone. Shall I .... it up for you?
2. I've eaten too much. I think I'll need to loosen my ....
3. I undid the top three .... of my shirt because it was so hot in the room.
4. I think it's a good idea to wear a money .... when you're travelling.
5. A button .... off my coat last night. Do you think you could sew it back on, please?
6. I can't .... the top button of my jeans. I think it's time I went on a diet.
7. When I got home, I .... my belt, took off my trousers and went straight to bed.
8. One of my shirt .... is missing. You haven't seen it lying around, have you?

Note
We use the word 'flies' for the zip at the front of trousers:
Psssst! Your flies are undone!
XYZ = Examine your zip!

bag

a shopping bag   a weekend bag   a shoulder bag   a handbag   a plastic bag   a clutch bag

1. Verb + bag

Complete the sentences with the correct form of the above verbs:

1. I tried to . . . . the biggest of the bags, but I wasn't strong enough.
2. Can I . . . . those bags for you? They look heavy.
3. I'm afraid that some of the eggs broke when I . . . . the bag getting out of the car.
4. A young shop assistant helped me to . . . . my bags at the supermarket checkout.
5. I . . . . the contents of my handbag on the table, but my missing earring wasn't there.

2. Common expressions

Match the halves:

1. It's OK. I can carry both bags.
2. I put my dirty washing into a plastic bag,
3. She's left her handbag
4. My mobile and my palmtop fit easily
5. Could you watch my bags
6. I've looked twice in my bag for the car keys,
7. He arrived, carrying a large bag of clothes

a. into my handbag.
b. but they're not there.
c. over his shoulder.
d. They're quite light.
e. lying open on the table.
f. and went to the launderette.
g. while I go to the toilet?

3. Bags at the airport

Complete the sentences with one of the above words:

1. Sorry we're so late. There was a . . . . with the bags from our flight.
2. I don't think we need to . . . . in this bag. It only weighs about 5 kilos.
3. One of our bags went . . . . at Paris while we changed planes for Athens.
4. They . . . . all my bags when I went through customs at Heathrow yesterday.

wallet

Common expressions

forget your wallet
put your wallet (somewhere)
leave your wallet behind

take money out of your wallet
my wallet was stolen
carry (your credit cards) in your wallet

Common expressions

Complete the sentences with the correct form of the above verbs:

1. When I got home from the restaurant, I realised that I had . . . . my wallet behind.
2. My wallet was . . . . from my pocket while I was travelling on the metro.
3. I . . . . a picture of my wife and son in my wallet along with all my cards.
4. Mel . . . . a £20 note out of his wallet and paid the taxi driver.
5. I . . . . my wallet, but Henry lent me the money to get into the cinema.
6. I can't remember where I . . . . my wallet. Has anyone seen it lying around?

Note   As a rule, men carry *wallets*. Women carry *purses*.

carry a wallet   pay by credit card   take money out   a purse

card

Common expressions

exchange business cards
carry a donor card
use a phone card

pay by credit card
pay by debit card
show your identity card

Common expressions

Complete the sentences with the correct kind of card:

1. I prefer to pay by . . . . card than by . . . . card. With . . . . cards you don't have to pay till the end of the month, but with . . . . cards, the money comes out of your account straightaway.
2. Do you know that it's much cheaper to make international calls if you use a . . . . card?
3. We exchanged . . . . cards at the beginning of the meeting.
4. We have to show our . . . . cards to the guard at the gate when we arrive in the morning.
5. I've always carried a . . . . card. I like to think that if I die in an accident, my heart and other organs will be useful to someone else.

Note   We send cards to each other on special occasions:
I must remember to send Carol a birthday card. She's 30 next month.
Thank you for the card. It was really nice of you to remember!

key

Verb + key	Common expressions
lose / find your keys	a spare key
mislay your keys	a bunch of keys
put your keys (in your pocket)	your car / house keys
hide a key (in a drawer)	the wrong key
hand in / return your key (to reception)	keep (the files) under lock and key
get a key cut	turn the key in the lock

1. Verb + key

Complete the sentences with the correct form of the above verbs:

1. I've hunted all over the house for my keys, but I can't . . . . them anywhere.
2. Try to remember where you . . . . the keys!
3. We forgot to . . . . in the keys when we checked out of the hotel!
4. I don't have a key to give Harry. I'll need to get one . . . .
5. I've . . . . a key under a flower pot by the door so that Jane can let herself in when she arrives from the airport.
6. When I . . . . my car keys, it was a disaster. It took days before I got a new set.
7. I seem to have . . . . my car keys. You haven't seen them lying around, have you?

2. Common expressions

Match the halves:

1. A bunch of keys fell out of her bag	a. I'm not sure who they belong to.
2. Leave a spare house key with a neighbour	b. It can't be the right one.
3. The cash box is kept under lock and key	c. in case you lock yourself out.
4. I picked up the wrong keys at the party.	d. when she opened it.
5. I can't turn this key in the lock.	e. in the secretary's office.

Note   You keep your keys on a *keyring*.

ring

Common expressions	
wear a ring	show off your ring
value a ring (at £100)	a ring fits you
the ring belonged to (your mother)	a gold / diamond ring
an engagement / a wedding ring	

Common expressions

Complete the sentences with the correct form of the above verbs:

1. This isn't a valuable ring, but it has great sentimental value. It . . . . to my grandmother.
2. I'm married, but like many British men I don't . . . . a wedding ring.
3. She couldn't wait to meet all her friends and . . . . off her diamond engagement ring.
4. My father's 24-carat gold ring was . . . . at £300, but I couldn't bring myself to sell it.
5. My wedding ring doesn't . . . . me any longer. I now have to wear it on my little finger.

glasses

Verb + glasses	**Common expressions**
wear glasses	sunglasses
put your glasses on	reading glasses
have your glasses on	thick glasses
take your glasses off	a pair of glasses
(you) need glasses	can't see without your glasses
break your glasses	

1. Verb + glasses

Complete the sentences with the correct form of the above verbs:

1. I have to . . . . my glasses on to see the television.
2. Many young people don't like . . . . glasses, and much prefer contact lenses.
3. I accidentally sat on my glasses and . . . . them. I don't have a spare pair!
4. He . . . . off his glasses and rubbed his eyes.
5. I couldn't really see what happened because I didn't . . . . my glasses on.
6. I'm beginning to have trouble reading small print. I think I . . . . glasses. I'll have to go for an eye test soon.

2. Common expressions

Match the halves:

1. I can't see without my glasses.	a. wear very thick glasses.
2. It's always a good idea to	b. wear sunglasses?
3. Why do security men always	c. read the instructions on the jar.
4. I had to put on my reading glasses to	d. have two pairs of glasses.
5. My friend is short-sighted and has to	e. You'll have to read the menu out to me.

Notes
1. If it rains, your glasses can *steam up*.
2. If the doctor or optician asks you to *remove* your glasses, you take them off.

lenses

Common expressions		
contact lenses	soft / hard lenses	daily-wear lenses
coloured lenses	contact lens case	contact lens solution
soak your lenses	wear lenses	

Common expressions

Complete the sentences with one of the above words:

1. I changed from hard lenses to . . . . ones about 20 years ago!
2. I'm thinking of trying some . . . . lenses. I've always wanted to have blue eyes!
3. I wish I could get lens . . . . in smaller bottles for when I travel.
4. I used to use monthly lenses, but now I use . . . . ones. A new pair every day cuts down the risk of infection.
5. You really need to . . . . your lenses for at least 6 hours before . . . . them again.

umbrella

Verb + umbrella	
put up / open an umbrella	put down your umbrella
hold an umbrella	take an umbrella
remember to bring an umbrella	forget your umbrella
lose your umbrella	

Verb + umbrella

Complete these sentences with the correct form of the above verbs:

1. You can .... the umbrella down now. I think it's stopped raining.
2. That's the second umbrella I've .... this year! I must have left it on the train.
3. It's starting to rain. It's a good job I remembered to .... an umbrella.
4. You'd better .... an umbrella with you – the forecast is for rain this afternoon.
5. It was difficult to .... the umbrella in the strong wind.
6. I left the office in a hurry and .... my umbrella.
7. It started to rain, so Hilda stopped to .... up her umbrella.

watch

Verb + watch	Common expressions
wear a watch	your watch is (5 minutes) fast / slow
put on / take off your watch	your watch gains / loses (5 minutes)
look at / glance at your watch	your watch beeps
set your watch (to the correct time)	your watch is under guarantee
your watch stops	a genuine / fake watch

1. Verb + watch

Complete the sentences with the correct form of the above verbs:

1. I .... at my watch and realised that I'd missed the last bus home.
2. My watch has .... I think it needs a new battery.
3. Tell me. How do you keep track of time if you don't .... a watch?
4. What time is it? I forgot to .... my watch on this morning.
5. I usually .... my watch to the time on the television or radio. It's the easiest way to make sure it's telling the right time.

2. Common expressions

Match the halves:

1. Sam's watch beeps every 15 minutes
2. My watch was 15 minutes fast
3. The watch is still under guarantee,
4. He says his watch is a genuine Rolex,
5. My grandfather's watch isn't very accurate.

a. but I know it's a fake he bought on holiday.
b. so they should repair it free of charge.
c. It loses about ten minutes every day.
d. and the noise is beginning to annoy me.
e. so I was early for the meeting.

Notes
1. A watch which you wear on your wrist is a *wrist watch*. Some people have a *pocket watch*.
2. Most watches today are *digital*. A traditional watch has *hands* which tell the time.
3. If you can wear your watch in the sea, it must be *waterproof*.

Test 16

| pocket | belt | button | zip | bag | wallet | card | key | ring | glasses | lenses | umbrella | watch |

1. Identifying the key word

Choose the key word which collocates with these verbs, adjectives and nouns:

1. . . . . carry, heavy, plastic, shopping
2. . . . . hold, put up, put down, take
3. . . . . come off, sew on, missing, top
4. . . . . carry, forget, stolen
5. . . . . wear, fit, diamond, wedding
6. . . . . wear, take off, reading, pair
7. . . . . mislay, spare, wrong, bunch
8. . . . . empty, back, inside, hole
9. . . . . carry, pay by, use, identity
10. . . . . wear, soak, contact, soft
11. . . . . put on, glance at, stop, fast
12. . . . . tighten, unbuckle, wear, leather
13. . . . . do up, open, broken

2. The correct collocation

Choose the correct collocation:

1. Have you seen a *bunch / group* of keys anywhere?
2. My watch is *early / slow*. It loses 5 minutes a day!
3. His eyesight is very bad. That's why he has such *strong / thick* glasses.

3. Key word quiz

Complete each sentence with the correct key word:

1. I've eaten too much. I'll need to loosen my . . . .
2. Although I'm married, I don't wear a . . . .
3. Can you help me carry this . . . .? It's too heavy for me.
4. Make sure you empty your . . . . before putting your trousers in the washing machine.
5. I can't see without my . . . .
6. My . . . . was five minutes slow this morning.
7. I've mislaid my car . . . . somewhere. Have you seen them?
8. Could you a sew a . . . . on my coat for me?
9. I don't wear glasses any more. I've changed to . . . .
10. You can put down your . . . . now. It's stopped raining.
11. I can't do up this . . . . I think it's broken.
12. You need to show an identity . . . . to get into the building.
13. I carry a photograph of my wife and children in my . . . .

4. Prepositions

Choose the correct preposition to complete these expressions:

1. Can I pay *by / with* credit card?
2. There was a mix up *for / with* my bags at the airport and one of them had gone astray.
3. I glanced *at / to* my watch to see if it was time to leave.
4. We keep all the medicines in the house *in / under* lock and key for safety.
5. The ring belonged *to / with* my grandmother.

Section 17

The family

parent

<table>
<tr><td>Verb + parent</td><td>Verb + prep + parents</td><td>Adjective + parent</td></tr>
<tr><td>parents worry</td><td>live with (your) parents</td><td>an elderly parent</td></tr>
<tr><td>parents separate / split up</td><td>fall out with (your) parents</td><td>a single parent</td></tr>
<tr><td>parents get divorced</td><td>look after (your) parents</td><td>strict parents</td></tr>
<tr><td>please your parents</td><td>communicate with (your) ...</td><td>foster parents</td></tr>
<tr><td>meet (her) parents</td><td></td><td>working parents</td></tr>
<tr><td>parents bring you up</td><td></td><td></td></tr>
</table>

"I met Ben's parents for the first time at the weekend. They seemed very nice."

1. Verb + parent

Complete these sentences with the correct form of the above verbs:

1. My parents separated when I was two, then got . . . . when I was four. I was brought up by my mother. I only saw my dad at the weekends.
2. I . . . . my boyfriend's parents for the first time last week. They seem very nice.
3. It's nearly midnight. I'd better phone home, or my parents will start to . . . .
4. I hate this dress, but I only wear it to . . . . my parents.
5. My parents . . . . me up to believe that the only way to be successful in life is to work hard.

2. Verb + with + parent

Match the halves:

1. I can't communicate with my parents.
2. My parents brought me up,
3. I've fallen out with my girlfriend again.
4. My wife and I lived with my parents until

a. but now I have to look after them!
b. we could afford a flat of our own.
c. They just don't understand me!
d. We haven't spoken to each other for a week.

3. Adjective + parent

Complete the sentences with the above adjectives:

1. Both my parents were very . . . . I wasn't allowed out after 7 o'clock until I was 16!
2. I have to take care of my . . . . parents. They're both in their eighties, and they need daily help with their housework and shopping.
3. Being a . . . . parent isn't easy. Bringing up a family on your own is hard work.
4. The meeting will be held in the school hall tomorrow evening to allow . . . . parents to attend.
5. My real parents died in a car crash when I was a baby. I was brought up by . . . . parents.

Note   Note these expressions:
I'm completely dependent on my parents for money.
I have a good relationship with my parents.
It is the parents' responsibility to make sure that their children attend school.

child / children

Verb + child	Adjective + child	Common expressions
have a child / children	a small / young child	ideal for children
bring up / raise children	grown-up children	(un)suitable for children
look after children	well-behaved children	happy as a child
teach children something	a gifted child	treat someone like a child
neglect children	an only child	
adopt children	a spoilt child	
children play together	the average child	
children tease each other		

1. Verb + child / children

Complete these sentences with the correct form of the above verbs:

1. My mother . . . . after the children every Monday. That's the day my wife is at the office.
2. I believe in right and wrong, and I intend to . . . . up my children to know the difference.
3. The children are out . . . . in the garden with their friends.
4. I was very fat when I was a child and the other children . . . . me about it. They called me names like 'Porky'. Children can be very cruel.
5. The children were taken into care by social services because their parents had started to . . . . them.
6. I think it is important that children are . . . . how to share with others.
7. Both our children are . . . . Sadly, we couldn't . . . . any children of our own.

2. Adjective + child / children

Complete the sentences with the above adjectives:

1. I'm an . . . . child. I often wish I had a brother or a sister.
2. The house is quiet these days. All of our children are . . . . and married now.
3. He has a wife and three . . . . children to support. The eldest is only 5.
4. Nowadays, the . . . . child spends about 20 hours a week watching television.
5. My brother is very clever. He goes to a special school for . . . . children.
6. Callum! Stop behaving like a . . . . child. You can't have everything you want!
7. The teacher gave the children a chocolate for being so . . . . at the school concert.

3. Common expressions

Match the halves:

1. I was very happy
2. The hotel has a leisure centre
3. The film contains a lot of violence
4. Would you stop treating me like a child!

a. and is ideal for children
b. I'm 16 and I can make up my own mind!
c. as a child.
d. and is unsuitable for young children.

Notes
1. Note the expression:
   Shaun won't understand – he's just a child!
2. Your *step-children* are the children of your partner's previous marriage.

Putting the children to bed!

wedding

Verb + wedding	Common expressions	Wedding + noun
go to a wedding	be a guest at a wedding	your wedding anniversary
invite (them) to the wedding	make a speech at a wedding	the wedding cake
have a big / quiet wedding	make a video of the wedding	the wedding dress
hold a wedding in a (church)	congratulations on your ...	a wedding invitation
call off the wedding		the wedding reception
pay for the wedding		a wedding ring

1. Verb + wedding

Complete these sentences with the correct form of the above verbs:

1. Jason and Elsa have . . . . us to their wedding next month.
2. My parents offered to help with our wedding, but Maria's parents are very traditional and wanted to . . . . for the wedding themselves.
3. I'm afraid we can't meet you this Saturday. We're . . . . to a friend's wedding.
4. We've decided to . . . . a quiet wedding, so we're only inviting the immediate families.
5. The wedding will be . . . . at St Patrick's Church on the 21st of May.
6. Francesca got cold feet and . . . . the wedding off at the last minute. Since then she's apologised to all the guests and returned their presents.

2. Common expressions:

Complete the sentences with one word from the above expressions:

1. As best man, I had to make a . . . . at my brother's wedding.
2. . . . . on your wedding anniversary. How many years is it now?
3. There were about 300 . . . . at our wedding.
4. We've hired a photographer, but we're also making a . . . . of the wedding.

3. Wedding + noun

Match the halves:

1. Hurry! The bride and groom are going to cut
2. I'm married, but I don't wear
3. Have you sent out
4. We went out to a restaurant to celebrate
5. We hired a local rock group to provide
6. The dishwasher was
7. You should have seen the wedding dress!

a. the music at our wedding reception.
b. a wedding present from my Uncle John.
c. It must have cost thousands!
d. the wedding invitations yet?
e. the wedding cake.
f. a wedding ring.
g. our first wedding anniversary.

*"I'll always wear my wedding ring.
And I'll always wear mine!"*

Note   A *honeymoon* is a short holiday that you go on immediately after the wedding:
We went to Rome for our honeymoon.
We stayed in a five-star hotel on our honeymoon.
All the guests wished the couple well as they left for their honeymoon.
Barbados is a popular destination for honeymoon couples.

husband, wife

Verb + husband / wife	Adjective + husband / wife
look for a husband / wife	your present husband / wife
meet your husband / wife	your ex- / former husband / wife
live with your husband / wife	your late husband / wife
leave your husband / wife	a loving husband / wife
lose your husband / wife	

1. Verb + husband / wife

Complete these sentences with the correct form of the above verbs:

1. My brother . . . . with his wife and two kids in Geneva.
2. I . . . . my wife last year. I've been very lonely since she died.
3. Have you heard that Margaret Duncan has . . . . her husband? She walked out on him after she found out he was having an affair.
4. I . . . . my wife at school when I was only 13. We got married when I was 18.
5. All my old school friends are married now, but I'm still . . . . for a wife!

2. Adjective + husband / wife

Complete the sentences with the above adjectives:

1. She's been married four times now. Her . . . . husband is 20 years younger than her!
2. Lawrence was a family man and a . . . . husband. We will all miss him.
3. My . . . . wife is now a millionaire. Sometimes I wish I hadn't divorced her!
4. These photographs bring back fond memories of my . . . . husband, Jack. They were taken on holiday the year before he died.

Notes   1. You can talk about your *first wife / her second husband*.
My first husband died of a heart attack when he was 35.

2. Your *late husband* means that he is dead.

funeral

Common expressions	
go to / attend a funeral	the funeral service is held (in a church)
wear black at a funeral	the funeral was a cremation
arrange a funeral	

Common expressions

Complete these sentences with one of the above words:

1. The funeral was . . . . last Friday morning. The actual funeral . . . . was wonderful.
2. In many countries, it is the custom to . . . . black at funerals.
3. As the eldest son, I had to . . . . my mother's funeral.
4. Hundreds of mourners . . . . the funeral of the two little boys who drowned in the river last week.
5. My uncle's funeral was a . . . . Everyone was surprised. The rest of his brothers and sisters were all buried.

Note   The people who attend a funeral are the *mourners*. A funeral is organised by a firm of *undertakers*.

baby

Verb + baby	Common expressions
be expecting a baby	a baby is born
have a baby	a baby sleeps
look after a baby	a baby cries
feed a baby	a baby plays with (toys)
hold a baby	the baby weighs (3) kilos
wake a baby	their baby is due (in August)
call the baby (John, Julia)	

1. Verb + baby

Complete these sentences with the correct form of the above verbs:

1. Did you hear that Janet . . . . a baby girl early this morning?
2. We're . . . . our first baby in August.
3. After the birth, Moira went back to work and her husband stayed at home to . . . . after the baby.
4. When I . . . . my tiny baby in my arms for the first time, I was so happy.
5. I went into the room very quietly, so as not to . . . . the baby.
6. We're thinking of . . . . the baby Unda after her grandmother.
7. I have to . . . . the baby every three or four hours. No wonder I'm so tired!

2. Common expressions

Complete these sentences with one of the above words:

1. I didn't get any sleep last night. The baby wouldn't stop . . . .
2. The baby only . . . . about 2 kilos at birth. He was born a month premature.
3. The baby was lying in her pram, ... with a rattle.
4. When's the baby . . . .? I heard it was January.
5. I don't really want to know the sex of my baby before it's . . . .
6. Try not to make too much noise. The baby's . . . .

birth

Common expressions	
give birth	be present at the birth
your birth certificate	the date / place / time of birth
congratulations on the birth of your (son, etc)	birth control

Common expressions

Match the halves:

1. Birth control is a very difficult issue,
2. My teacher has just given birth
3. My great-grandmother doesn't know her exact
4. Congratulations
5. It's now quite common for fathers to be present
6. I've lost my birth certificate. Do you know

a. how I can get a new one?
b. on the birth of your daughter!
c. especially in poor countries.
d. to twins, a boy and a girl.
e. date of birth. She thinks it's 1912.
f. at the birth of their children.

birthday

Common expressions	Birthday + noun
celebrate your birthday	a birthday cake
remember / forget a birthday	a birthday card
get a (bike) for your birthday	a birthday party
wish someone a happy birthday	a birthday present
have a party for someone's birthday	

1. Common expressions

Complete these sentences with the correct form of the above verbs:

1. We're .... a party for Faisal's 50th birthday. Would you like to come?
2. I'm .... my husband a digital camera for his birthday!
3. Let's go out for a meal to .... your birthday.
4. I'm sorry I .... your birthday. It just slipped my mind. Here's a card and a present.
5. Your grandmother can't come to your party, but she .... you a happy birthday and hopes you have a great day.

2. Birthday + noun

Complete the sentences with the above nouns:

1. Zaina blew out all 15 candles on her birthday ....
2. The necklace was a birthday .... from my husband.
3. I must remember to send Mikako a birthday .... I forgot last year.
4. Sheila has invited me to her son's 21st birthday ....

present

Verb + present	Adjective + present
buy a present	a lovely present
get a present	an expensive present
wrap / unwrap a present	a small present
thank someone for a present	a leaving present

1. Verb + present

Complete these sentences with the correct form of the above verbs:

1. Did you .... many presents for your birthday?
2. I can't wait to see my wife's face when she .... her present!
3. I must .... Mrs Auld for her wedding present. It was nice of her to think of us.
4. I'm not .... her a present. I don't know her that well. I'll just send a card.
5. We .... her present in silver paper and tied it with a red bow.

2. Adjective + present

Match the halves:

1. I've brought you a small present.
2. I got lots of lovely presents for Christmas,
3. Everyone in our class gave some money towards
4. Duncan got lots of expensive presents on his 21st.

a. but yours was the nicest!
b. His father bought him a car.
c. It's not much, but I think you'll like it.
d. a leaving present for the teacher.

Test 17

1. Identifying the key word

Choose the key word which collocates with these verbs, adjectives and nouns:

1. . . . .   be expecting, have, feed, hold
2. . . . .   celebrate, forget, cake, card
3. . . . .   give, certificate, control
4. . . . .   please, elderly, foster, single
5. . . . .   call off, go to, big, anniversary
6. . . . .   go to, arrange, hold
7. . . . .   buy, get, wrap, lovely
8. . . . .   adopt, bring up, have, spoilt
9. . . . .   meet, leave, loving, late

2. The correct collocation

Choose the correct collocation:

1. She's *an only / a single* parent. Her husband left her a year after they were married.
2. I'm *an only / a single* child. But I wish I had a brother or sister.
3. We wanted a *little / quiet* wedding so we only invited our families and closest friends.
4. Can you believe Sue is now back with her *former / early* husband again?
5. Have you heard the news? Pilar's *had / made* a baby boy!
6. Caroline *gave / made* birth to a beautiful baby girl early this morning.
7. I got a beautiful clock as a *goodbye / leaving* present when I retired last year.
8. She gave me a *good / lovely* present for my birthday.

3. Key word quiz

Complete each sentence with the correct key word:

1. How did you celebrate your . . . .? Did you have a party?
2. We adopted two . . . . after we found out we couldn't have any of our own.
3. Please remember to bring a copy of your . . . . certificate with you.
4. We'd like to invite you to our daughter's . . . . on the 28th of July.
5. Can you wrap Tom's . . . . ? There's some nice coloured paper in the drawer.
6. When my father died, I had to arrange the . . . .
7. We're expecting our first . . . . in June.
8. Elaine, have you met my . . . . , Mark?
9. My . . . . separated when I was only six. I only saw my father at weekends.

4. Prepositions

Choose the correct preposition to complete these expressions:

1. I was very happy *as / for* a child.
2. I had to make a speech *at / on* my brother's wedding.
3. The baby's due *in / on* December.
4. Congratulations *for / on* the birth of your daughter.
5. I wish *to you / you* a happy birthday.

Section 18

Health and sport

hospital

Common expressions

Complete the sentences with the correct form of the above verbs:

1. I'm . . . . into hospital next week for a small operation on my knee.
2. I went to A and E *(Accident and Emergency)* with pains in my chest, and they . . . . me in hospital overnight for tests.
3. Many of the people injured in the rail crash were . . . . at local hospitals.
4. My father's just . . . . out of hospital. He'll need extra care at home for a few weeks until he's fit enough to look after himself again.

Choose the correct preposition:

5. Our family want to thank all the doctors and nurses *at / in* the hospital.
6. During the holiday, I spent three days in hospital *for / with* food poisoning.
7. He was rushed to hospital *by / in* ambulance.
8. My mother is seriously ill *at / in* hospital at the moment.

Notes

1. Note this expression:
   The injured climber was airlifted to hospital. (taken by helicopter)
2. Another word for the Accident and Emergency department of a hospital is *Casualty.*
   I ended up in Casualty after falling off my motorbike.

doctor

Verb + doctor

Complete the sentences with the correct form of the above verbs:

1. Ramon has a very high temperature. Maybe we should . . . . the doctor?
2. The doctor . . . . some antibiotics for my throat infection.
3. I'd like to make an appointment to . . . . Dr Venters today, if possible?
4. If you have any kind of heart condition, you should . . . . your doctor before flying to New Zealand.
5. The doctor has . . . . me to an ear specialist at the Royal Infirmary.
6. The doctor . . . . the old woman carefully for signs of injury before she was lifted into the ambulance.

Notes

1. Doctors work at *surgeries* or in *clinics.*
2. The doctor you normally see is your *GP* (General Practitioner).

headache, cough, cold, virus

headache	cough	cold	virus
have (got) a ...	have a cough	catch a cold	pick up a virus
complain of a ...	coughs spread disease	have a cold	a nasty virus
it gives me a ...	a bad / nasty cough	shake off a cold	the virus causes (fever)
this relieves your ...	a persistent cough	a cold clears up	there's a virus going
headaches go away	cough medicine	a bad / heavy cold	round
a bad / splitting ...	cough sweets		

1. Expressions with headache

Complete the sentences with the correct form of the above verbs:

1. I've taken four paracetamol tablets, but my headache still hasn't . . . . away!
2. The noise of the traffic in the city centre has . . . . me a bad headache.
3. I've . . . . a splitting headache all day long, so I'm just going to bed.
4. Aspirin is very good at . . . . my headaches, but I don't really like taking painkillers on a regular basis.
5. She's been . . . . of a headache for two days now. I think she should make an appointment to see the doctor.

2. Expressions with cough

Match the halves:

1. I stopped taking my cough medicine
2. I wish I could get rid of this cough.
3. Cover your mouth with a tissue.
4. I've got a sore throat and a persistent cough
5. Have you got a cough sweet?

a. It's making me miserable.
b. I've got to give a talk in 5 minutes.
c. which just won't go away!
d. because it was making me feel sleepy.
e. Coughs and sneezes spread diseases!

"I've got a heavy cold and a splitting headache."

3. Expressions with cold

Complete the sentences with the correct form of the above verbs:

1. Don't come into work if you . . . . a heavy cold. It's better if you go to bed and rest.
2. I think I've . . . . a cold. I've been sneezing all morning.
3. Most coughs and colds . . . . up after a few days. So just drink lots of water and keep warm. You don't really need to take any medicine.
4. I've been trying to . . . . off this cold for weeks, but I can't seem to get rid of it!

4. Expressions with virus

Complete the sentences with the correct form of the above verbs:

1. There's a nasty virus . . . . round the college just now.
2. The virus . . . . stomach pains and diarrhoea. Make sure you drink plenty of water.
3. I . . . . up a nasty virus while I was on holiday. I was off work for weeks.

medicine, pill

Expressions with medicine	Expressions with pill
take medicine	a sleeping pill
give (him) medicine	a vitamin pill
keep your medicine (in a box)	take a pill
the medicine works / takes effect	swallow a pill
medicine makes you feel (drowsy / sleepy)	the doctor gives you pills
the medicine tastes awful	pills are addictive

1. Expressions with medicine

Complete the sentences with the correct form of one of the above verbs:

1. The doctor didn't . . . . me any medicine. She said the infection would clear up by itself.
2. In our house we . . . . all medicines in a locked cupboard in the bathroom.
3. I had to stop . . . . my medicine because it was making me sick.
4. The medicine . . . . me feel drowsy, so I couldn't drive while I was taking it.
5. The medicine . . . . awful! I can only take it mixed with some orange juice.
6. Don't expect the medicine to . . . . effect immediately. It could take a week or two.

2. Expressions with pill

Match the halves:

1. My grandfather keeps forgetting
2. The doctor gave me some pills
3. I don't like taking sleeping pills regularly.
4. I find it really difficult to swallow these pills
5. I don't take vitamin pills.

a. for the pain in my legs.
b. I just make sure I eat lots of fresh food.
c. because they taste awful!
d. They can become addictive.
e. to take his pills.

"These pills make me feel sleepy."

Note   Note that *the Pill* refers to the contraceptive pill:
Mandy has gone on the Pill. She says she's not ready to start a family yet.

injection

Verb + injection	
have an injection	need an injection
an injection hurts you	give someone an injection (in the arm)

Verb + injection

Complete the sentences with the correct form of the above verbs:

1. I was a little embarrassed when the nurse . . . . me an injection in my bottom.
2. The injection didn't . . . . at all. I just felt a slight prick.
3. Like most children, my son hates . . . . injections.
4. I . . . . a tetanus injection after I was bitten by a dog on the beach last summer.

blood

Common expressions

Match the halves:

1. I'm a regular blood donor.
2. She lost a lot of blood
3. We'll need to do some blood tests
4. I asked the doctor to
5. There was blood
6. The sight of blood always
7. The police were able to identify
8. What's the matter with your head?

a. in the accident.
b. the killer from his blood-stained shirt.
c. pouring down his face from a head wound.
d. makes me feel sick and faint.
e. to find out what's making you feel so tired.
f. check my blood pressure.
g. It's covered in blood!
h. Have you ever given blood yourself?

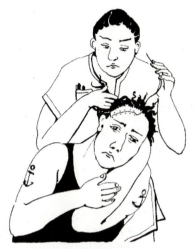

*"You should have seen the blood!
I needed 10 stitches!"*

bandage, stitches, x-ray

Common expressions

Complete the sentences with the correct form of the above verbs:

1. The cut over my right eye . . . . 10 stitches.
2. He . . . . his bandage, and showed me the cut on his leg.
3. After the accident, I had to . . . . an x-ray of my foot to see if any bones were broken.
4. It's quite a deep cut, so we'll need to . . . . a bandage on it.
5. The doctors still don't know what's wrong with me. Nothing . . . . up on the x-ray.
6. When do you . . . . your stitches out?
7. I had to . . . . my teeth and gums x-rayed. That's the first time for 4 years!

ball

Verb + ball		
play with a ball	throw a ball	catch a ball
bounce a ball	a ball rolls	miss the ball

Verb + ball

Complete the sentences with the correct form of the above verbs:

1. Jordan . . . . the ball two or three times, then threw it into the basketball net.
2. I watched the children . . . . with a ball in the park.
3. The baby's ball . . . . across the floor and went under the chair.
4. I swung the bat wildly at the ball, but I completely . . . . it!
5. See if you can . . . . the ball when I . . . . it to you. Try not to drop it.

Notes

1. If I *throw the ball to* you, I want you to *catch* it. However if I *throw a ball at* you, I'm trying to hit you!
2. In a game of football, you can't *touch* the ball, but you can *kick* it, *head* it or *pass* it:
   I'm sure he was trying to kick me and not the ball. He's a really dirty player!
   Hartson jumped above all the other players and headed the ball past the goalkeeper into the net.
   He's a really greedy player. He never passes the ball!

football

Common expressions	**Football + noun**
play football	football boots
watch football	football fans
be mad / crazy about football	a football strip
be good at football	a football match
be useless at football	a football player
	a football team
	a football pitch

1. Common expressions

Match the halves:

1. At school, I was useless at football.	a. but not good enough to play professionally.
2. Do you play any other sports	b. He's never missed a match in ten years.
3. Jim's not here. He's gone home	c. That's why I was never picked for the team.
4. My friend, Alan, is crazy about football.	d. besides football?
5. Our eldest son is very good at football,	e. to watch the football on TV.

2. Football + noun

Complete these sentences with the above nouns:

1. Which football . . . . do you support?
2. My dad took me to watch my first football . . . . when I was only 2 years old.
3. The Brazilian, Ronaldinho, was voted best football . . . . in the world in 2004.
4. There's a football . . . . at the end of the road, where kids practise most nights.
5. Thousands of football . . . . invaded the pitch at the end of the cup final.
6. I wash my own football . . . . after a game and I also clean my football . . . .

score, result

Common expressions

Match the halves:

1. The match ended in a draw.
2. 1–0 to Greece! What a surprise result!
3. Do you know the latest score
4. Last night's result was very disappointing.
5. They are both strong teams, so it's difficult

a. in the match between Lazio and AC Milan?
b. The final score was one-all. (1–1)
c. Everyone expected France to win easily.
d. to predict the result of tonight's match.
e. It means we're out of the competition.

player

Common expressions	Adjective + player
players beat / defeat other players	a competitive player
players earn (lots of) money	an experienced player
players warm up	an exciting player
players sign autographs	a great player
football players score goals	
clubs sign / buy new players	

1. Common expressions

Complete the sentences with the correct form of the above verbs:

1. Players from both teams were . . . . autographs outside the stadium before the game.
2. Our best player was easily . . . . by the Russian, Sharapova.
3. He might be our star player, but he hasn't . . . . a goal for nearly ten matches!
4. FC Roma have . . . . two new players this year.
5. We arrived early to watch the players . . . . up before the match.
6. Many football players . . . . a lot of money. Some are paid as much as £60,000 a week!

2. Adjective + player

Complete the sentences with the correct form of the above adjectives.

1. I think Pelé was the . . . . football player of all time.
2. McEnroe was a highly . . . . tennis player who hated losing.
3. The team has some young players, but it also has a number of more . . . . ones.
4. Ronaldo is a really . . . . player. He is absolutely wonderful to watch.

Test 18

1. Identifying the key word

Choose the key word which collocates best with these verbs, adjectives and nouns:

health

1.	heavy, catch, shake off
2.	see, call, consult
3.	need, have, hurt
4.	nasty, persistent
5.	go into, be taken to
6.	put on, remove
7.	makes you drowsy
8.	pick up, go round, nasty
9.	have, need, show up on
10.	swallow, vitamin, sleeping
11.	have, go away, splitting
12.	need, get, ten
13.	give, lose, pressure

sport

14.	play, watch, match
15.	predict, surprise
16.	hear, final, latest
17.	bounce, throw, catch
18.	competitive, experienced

2. Key word quiz

Complete each sentence with the correct key word:

health

1. Consult your .... if you still have the headache tomorrow.
2. He had a nasty cut on his head and .... was running down his face.
3. Will you try to be quiet! I've got a splitting ....
4. The .... the doctor gave me for my cough is making me sleepy.
5. The cut on your leg is quite deep. I think you'll need some ....
6. I'm going into .... next week for an operation on my foot.
7. I've got this persistent .... which I can't seem to get rid of.
8. They're big .... so you'll need some water to help you swallow them.
9. I thought I had broken a small bone in my hand, but nothing showed up on the ....
10. My nose is running and I feel hot. I think I've caught a ....
11. The nurse gave me a tetanus .... in my arm.
12. There's a nasty .... going round at the moment. Make sure you wash your hands.
13. We'll need to put a .... on that cut, so that it doesn't become infected.

sport

14. He bounced the .... three times before throwing it to me.
15. It's difficult to predict the .... but I think Chelsea will win.
16. The final .... was 3–3.
17. I think professional football .... earn too much money.
18. I'd rather watch .... than play it.

Section 19

Education

school

Verb + school	School + noun	Common expressions
go to / attend school	your school days	be at school
start school (at 5)	the school hall	be late for school
leave school (at 18)	your school report	be absent from school
miss school	school rules	stay behind after school
change schools	a school trip	all through school
collect (them) from school	school uniform	
be expelled from school	school work	
play truant from school		

1. Verb + school

Complete the sentences with the correct form of the above verbs:

1. I didn't do very well at high school. I . . . . school at 16 with no qualifications.
2. In the UK, children . . . . primary school when they are 4 or 5 years old.
3. I . . . . a lot of school through illness last year. I might have to repeat the year.
4. My wife's ill, so I'll have to leave work early today to . . . . the children from school.
5. My father's a diplomat, so I have to . . . . schools every time he moves to a new country!
6. Ed Savage was . . . . from school for attacking the history teacher with a knife.
7. We've just discovered that Tom has been . . . . truant from school. We had no idea!
8. I didn't . . . . the same school as my sister. She . . . . to a high school for girls.

2. School + noun

Match the halves:

1. Our class is going on a school trip
2. Smoking is against
3. I've fallen behind with
4. The parents' evening on June 26th will be held
5. My school reports always said the same thing –
6. School uniform is compulsory in my school.
7. Why do adults say that your school days are

a. in the school hall.
b. 'Could try harder'!
c. There's no choice. You have to wear it.
d. to Germany this year.
e. the school rules.
f. the happiest days of your life?
g. my school work again.

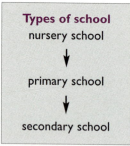

Types of school

nursery school

↓

primary school

↓

secondary school

3. Common expressions

Complete the sentences with the correct preposition:

1. Hurry up or we'll be late . . . . school.
2. Both my children are still . . . . school. The eldest is 17.
3. Anna's very clever. She got A grades all the way . . . . high school.
4. Patricia's been absent . . . . school for over a month now.
5. I had to stay behind . . . . school. My guidance teacher wanted to speak to me about why I'd been late four days this week.

teacher

"Although he was strict, he was always a very enthusiastic teacher!"

1. Verb + teacher

Complete the sentences with the correct form of the above verbs:

1. Our English teacher always . . . . our grammar and spelling in class.
2. Our maths teacher . . . . our exam papers, and went over the answers.
3. My teacher . . . . me off for being late again.
4. I want to . . . . a drama teacher when I leave school.
5. The geography teacher . . . . us how to read a map.
6. When I was at school, the teachers used to . . . . us for even small things. Nowadays teachers have different attitudes.

2. Adjective + teacher

Match the halves:

1. Our new teacher has no
2. Mo went back to her old school
3. Mrs Lloyd really knows her subject.
4. David would make a good teacher.
5. The new teacher is enthusiastic.
6. I had some awful teachers at school.
7. I think teachers have to be strict so that

a. He has a lot of patience.
b. One couldn't even spell correctly!
c. the students know what the rules are.
d. control over the class.
e. to visit some of her former teachers.
f. She's so full of ideas.
g. She's an excellent teacher.

Notes

1. A *supply teacher* teaches the class when the normal teacher is off sick.
2. Note these expressions:
   Jeremy's working in a restaurant, but he's a teacher by profession.
   Pam applied to university on the advice of her teacher.
3. To *become a teacher*, you go to *teacher training college* where you *train as a teacher*. Then you *qualify as a teacher*.
4. You can be a *primary teacher* or a *secondary teacher*.

student

Student + verb	Adjective + student	Common expressions
students are taught	an angry student	students do (French)
students graduate	a bright / brilliant student	students adapt to
students drop out	a hard-working student	(university) life
students are bullied	a lazy student	students find
	your fellow students	accommodation
	a former student	students have debts
	a full-time / part-time ...	student discounts

1. Verb + student

Complete the sentences with the correct form of the above verbs:

1. Our students are . . . . through lectures, seminars and individual tutorials.
2. I hated school because I was . . . . by some of the other students.
3. About 90% of our students . . . . from university with degrees. Unfortunately, the other 10% . . . . out after their first year.

2. Adjective + student

Complete the sentences with the above adjectives:

1. Eva is a . . . . student – she should get a first-class degree.
2. Hundreds of . . . . students held demonstrations in the university square to protest about the cuts in education.
3. Greg is a very hard-working student. He's also extremely popular with his . . . . students.
4. I retired from teaching many years ago, but I still get cards from my . . . . students.
5. I'm a . . . . student at the moment, but I'm thinking of going part-time because I'm finding it difficult to pay for the course, my food and accommodation.
6. Colin's a very . . . . student – he's never handed in an essay on time!

3. Common expressions:

Match the halves:

1. Some students have difficulty
2. Students get a 10% discount
3. It's difficult for students to find
4. In the UK, some students have huge debts
5. Most of the students at my college are

a. on all books in the store.
b. adapting to college life away from home.
c. by the time they graduate from university.
d. doing business courses.
e. somewhere nice to live in some cities.

"She's one of the most hard-working students I've ever met."

Note   Note these types of student:
The college library has facilities for disabled students.
The university has a large number of overseas students. Many of them are from China.
There are a number of mature students living on campus. Some have children.

class and lesson

Expressions with class	Verb + lesson
teach a class	prepare a lesson
attend a class	give lessons
miss a class	go to lessons
be in the same class as (her)	enjoy a lesson
pay attention in class	have a lesson (on pollution)
be top / bottom of the class	spend the lesson (writing, reading)

1. Expressions with class

Match the halves:

1. If Tanya paid more attention in class,
2. Heather and I are old friends.
3. Jenny was the brightest student.
4. Our teacher was absent, so the headmaster
5. I missed my class this morning
6. He got into trouble when his father

a. found out he wasn't attending classes.
b. because I had to go to the dentist.
c. taught the class.
d. She was always top of the class.
e. she'd get better marks in her tests.
f. I was in the same class as her at school.

2. Verb + lesson

Complete the sentences with the correct form of the above verbs:

1. I . . . . most of my lessons at school, but I find maths dead boring.
2. One of my students asked me if I could . . . . her private English lessons after school.
3. Physics was boring today. We . . . . the whole lesson copying from the blackboard!
4. My mother has started . . . . to French lessons at the local college in the evening.
5. We . . . . a lesson on the Spanish Civil War in history today.
6. As a teacher, I usually spend Sunday evening marking essays and . . . . my lessons for the following week.

Note   You can have *driving, piano, singing, golf, dancing, private lessons:*
I can't meet you till after my piano lesson at 5.
I've started going to dancing lessons.

test

Verb + test		
do / sit / take a test	pass / fail a test	mark a test
cheat in a test	revise for a test	

Verb + test

Complete the sentences with the correct form of the above verbs:

1. Paul Henly sits behind me in class and he always . . . . in tests. He looks over my shoulder and tries to copy my answers.
2. We all did badly in the test. Only two people in the class managed to . . . . !
3. I stayed in all weekend because I had to . . . . for my biology test.
4. We don't know the results yet. Our teacher hasn't finished . . . . our test.
5. At the end of each month, we . . . . a progress test to see how much we have learned.

book

Verb + book	Adjective + book	Noun + of + book	Expressions
read a book	a good book	a chapter of a book	browse through a ...
write a book	a long / short book	a copy of a book	read a book from
open / close a book	an interesting book	a page of a book	cover to cover
finish a book	a boring book	the title of a book	lend a book to (him)
enjoy a book	the book is heavy-	the author of a book	borrow a book from
	going	a pile of books	(him)

1. Verb + book

Complete these sentences with the correct form of the above verbs:

1. Our science teacher has . . . . several textbooks on chemistry teaching.
2. My eyes were tired, so I . . . . the book and put it down on the bedside table.
3. I'm nowhere near . . . . the book – I'm only half-way through it!
4. I'm . . . . a book on Japanese history at the moment.
5. I . . . . the book you gave me for my birthday. It had a really good ending.

2. Adjective + book

Complete the sentence with the correct from of the above adjectives:

1. It took me over a month to read *War and Peace!* I think it's the . . . . book I've ever read.
2. It was such a . . . . book. I finished it in a day! I just couldn't put it down!
3. I don't know how anyone could be interested in such a . . . . book. I gave up on page 2!
4. All these books look so . . . . , I don't know which one to choose!
5. The book on globalisation you gave me was rather . . . . I gave up half-way through it. There was too much information in it for me to take in.

3. Noun + of + book

Complete the sentences with the above nouns:

1. I'm on the last . . . . of the book, so I'll finish it before lunch. I've only 5 pages left to go.
2. What's the . . . . of William Boyd's new book?
3. J K Rowling is the well-known . . . . of the Harry Potter series.
4. There was a . . . . of books on top of the table.
5. I can't find a . . . . of the book anywhere. All the shops have sold out.
6. I only managed to read two . . . . of my book before I fell asleep.

4. Common expressions:

Match the halves:

1. I only dipped into the book,
2. Don't ask Jane for her copy of 'Hamlet'.
3. I browsed through the books in the library,
4. I'm afraid I borrowed your course book

a. but I couldn't find one I liked.
b. without asking.
c. She doesn't like lending anybody her books.
d. but Liz read it from cover to cover – twice!

Notes

1. Note these ways of saying someone is very interested in a book:
   William was so engrossed in his book that he didn't hear me come in.
   William was completely lost in his book.

2. Note that 'book' can refer to the phonebook:
   Give me a call – my number's in the book.
   Look up his number in the book.

page

Verb + page	Adjective + page	Common expressions
read a page	the front / back page	be on page (33)
turn the page (over)	a blank page	be over the page
tear out a page	the opposite page	open your book at page (27)
photocopy a page	a new page	turn to page (65)
		read the words on the page
		be at the top / bottom of the page

"I can't read the print on this page. It's too small!"

"Just one more page and then you're going to bed!"

1. Verb + page

Match the halves:

1. She's a slow reader. It takes her about 5 minutes
2. I've only read 30 pages of the book so far,
3. The library will charge you 5p
4. Someone's torn out two pages from this book.

a. but I hope to finish it by next week.
b. How can anybody be so selfish?
c. to turn a page!
d. for each page you photocopy.

2. Adjective + page

Complete the sentences with the above adjectives:

1. Write your full name on the . . . . page of the examination paper.
2. I just sat in the exam and stared at the . . . . page in front of me. I couldn't think of anything to write.
3. Write the answer to each question on a . . . . page.
4. Read the text on the left-hand page carefully, then complete the diagram on the . . . . page.

3. Preposition focus

Complete these sentences with the correct preposition:

1. The answers to this exercise are . . . . page 102 at the back of your book.
2. Open your books . . . . page 45, and do exercises 1, 2 and 3.
3. Turn . . . . page 88 and complete the reading task.
4. I can't read the words . . . . this page. The print is too small.
5. The answers are . . . . the page, but don't look until you've finished the exercise!
6. Write your name and class at the top . . . . each page.

Notes
1. Note that we use 'page' to talk about information we get on the internet:
   I'm doing a course at college on how to design web pages.
   Do you want the address of my home page?
   To see the next page, click 'forward'. To view the last page, click 'back'.
2. Note that we talk about *a page of a book*, but *a sheet of paper.*

Test 19

school	teacher	student	class	lesson	test	book	page

1. Identifying the key word

Choose the key word which collocates with these verbs, adjectives and nouns:

1. . . . .   read, turn, new, blank
2. . . . .   attend, be top of, miss, teach
3. . . . .   attend, leave, change, rules
4. . . . .   do, mark, pass, revise for
5. . . . .   graduate, bright, hard-working, full-time
6. . . . .   give, have, enjoy, prepare
7. . . . .   teach, enthusiastic, former, strict
8. . . . .   read, write, boring, good

2. Choose the correct collocation

Choose the correct collocation:

1. A friend of mine was *banned* / *expelled* from school for hitting the teacher with a book.
2. I'd like to *become* / *make* a teacher after I leave school.
3. Many students never finish their courses. They drop *off* / *out* after a few months.
4. I've *lost* / *missed* a lot of classes this week.
5. The history teacher, Mr Wilson, *did* / *gave* a great lesson on ancient Egypt today.
6. We *did* / *made* a maths test yesterday and I failed again!
7. Key Words is actually quite a good *name* / *title* for a book for English students, isn't it?
8. Quite often there are *blank* / *empty* pages at the end of a book.

3. Key word quiz

Complete each sentence with the correct key word:

1. At school, Jane was a brilliant . . . . – always top of the class.
2. I spend about two hours every evening preparing all my . . . . for the next day.
3. I'll have to stay in this weekend. I have to revise for my chemistry . . . . on Monday.
4. Can I photocopy two . . . . from this book, please?
5. He's a terrible . . . . I've learnt almost nothing since I joined his class.
6. Pauline! You're day-dreaming again. I wish you would pay more attention in . . . .
7. Mr Hill gave the most brilliant English . . . . today. It was really interesting.
8. In the UK, you can leave . . . . at 16, but many students stay on until they are 18.

4. Prepositions

Choose the correct preposition to complete these expressions:

1. I was late *at* / *for* school today. I missed the bus.
2. Some students find it difficult to adapt *to* / *with* life away from home.
3. We had a really good lesson *in* / *on* global warming in geography today.
4. The teacher gave no marks to my friend, Pete, because he cheated *at* / *in* the test.
5. I think he's in the library browsing *among* / *through* the books.
6. My eyes were tired and it was difficult to read the words *in* / *on* the page.

Section 20

Reading and writing

newspaper

Verb + newspaper	Common expressions	Noun + of + newspaper
buy a newspaper	work as a (journalist) on a	a copy of (today's) newspaper
read a newspaper	newspaper	the front / back page of the
glance through a newspaper	sell your story to a	newspaper
recycle your newspapers	newspaper	the (business, sports) section
(stories) are reported in a	finish with the newspaper	of the newspaper
(local / national) newspaper	read something in the	a sheet of newspaper
	newspapers	

1. Verb + newspaper

Complete these sentences with the correct form of the above verbs:

1. I try not to put newspapers and empty bottles in the rubbish bin. I think it's much better to
   . . . . them.
2. I only had time to . . . . through the newspaper before I left for work. I didn't have time
   to read it properly.
3. I've stopped . . . . a daily newspaper because I never seem to find the time to
   . . . . it!
4. The story about the Prince's car accident was . . . . in *The Times* and all the other
   national papers.

2. Common expressions

Complete the sentences with the correct preposition:

1. Maria, have you finished . . . . the newspaper yet?
2. The footballer's ex-girlfriend made a fortune selling her story . . . . the newspapers.
3. I don't believe everything I read . . . . the newspapers.
4. He's now the editor of the *Daily Mail*, but he began his career as a journalist . . . .
   a local newspaper in Wales.

3. Noun + of + newspaper

Match the halves:

1. The Queen's picture is on	a. the business section of the newspaper.
2. The sports news is usually on	b. sheets of newspaper on the floor.
3. You'll find today's exchange rates in	c. the front pages of all the newspapers today.
4. Before I started painting the room I put	d. a copy of yesterday's newspaper?
5. Have you got	e. the back pages of the newspaper.

Notes

1. We say something is *published / is reported / appears* in a newspaper:
   Ivan's story was published / was reported in the local paper.
   The story first appeared in our local paper.
2. Note these expressions:
   Most newspapers are now available online.
   What do the papers say about the war?
3. Note these different kinds of newspaper:

a daily newspaper	*an evening newspaper*	*a Sunday newspaper*
today's newspaper	*a national newspaper*	*a local newspaper*
a quality newspaper	*a popular newspaper*	*a tabloid newspaper*

4. The following are ways of talking about the politics of a newspaper:

a left-wing newspaper	*an independent newspaper*	*a right-wing newspaper*

magazine

1. Verb + magazine

Complete these sentences with the correct form of the above verbs:

1. I . . . . several magazines to . . . . on the train.
2. *Manjo* is a popular music magazine which is . . . . at teenagers.
3. The film star, Brad Wartz, was very angry when *Goodbye* magazine . . . . pictures of him at a private party in LA.
4. I'm a freelance journalist. I . . . . for a number of different fashion magazines.
5. I . . . . to several monthly magazines. It's much cheaper than buying the magazine every month from a shop.

2. Noun + of + magazine

Complete the sentences with the above nouns:

1. Our local newsagent stocks a wide . . . . of magazines.
2. This month Kylie Minogue is featured on the front . . . . of *Vogue* magazine.
3. In his last job, Henry was the . . . . of a popular men's magazine.
4. Have you read the current . . . . of *Time* magazine? It's got a good article on China.
5. You can buy the Pavarotti DVD at half price. This special offer is only open to the . . . . of this magazine.

3. Common expressions:

Match the halves:

1. The free magazine from the bank gives
2. She lay on the sofa,
3. The women's magazines
4. The perfume has been advertised in
5. There's an interesting article

a. are all on the middle shelf over there.
b. all the popular women's magazines.
c. lots of useful hints on how to save money.
d. on Bill Clinton in this month's *Hello* magazine.
e. leafing through fashion magazines.

"There's nothing to read in them! I just leaf through them to see what's in fashion!"

Note   Magazines and newspapers sometimes have *supplements* – separate sections on one topic:
There's a great property supplement in The Scotsman *on Thursdays.*
The sports supplement in Sunday's Telegraph *was really interesting.*
*The Times *has a really interesting supplement on holidays today.*

pen and pencil

Expressions with pen	Expressions with pencil
write with a (black) pen	use a pencil
mark with a red pen	sharpen your pencil
pick up / put down your pen	break your pencil
hold your pen	write in pencil
borrow / lend a pen	draw in pencil
your pen doesn't work / write	a sharp / blunt pencil
fill out / in a form in pen	coloured pencils
ballpoint pen	a pencil sharpener
fountain pen	

1. Expressions with pen

Match the halves:

1. Please fill out the application form
2. My pen has stopped working.
3. The teacher had marked
4. I was so nervous
5. Can you lend me a pen please?
6. Ballpoint pens are cheap
7. Please stop writing

   a. I've forgotten to bring one today.
   b. I could hardly hold my pen.
   c. and aren't as messy as fountain pens.
   d. Have you got a spare one I could borrow?
   e. and put down your pens.
   f. in pen, not pencil.
   g. all my mistakes with a red pen.

2. Expressions with pencil

Complete these sentences with one of the above words:

1. I pressed too hard on the paper, and . . . . my pencil.
2. My brother uses his penknife to . . . . his pencil. I use a pencil . . . .
3. When I was at school, we always . . . . in pencil. When we had finished something, we then wrote it out in ink.
4. I can't write with this pencil – it's . . . . ! Have you got a . . . . one?
5. Children don't . . . . pencils and rubbers any more. They all have pens.
6. It's best to . . . . in pencil first. That way it's easy to make changes to your drawing.

Notes

1. We say *my pen isn't working*, but not *my pencil isn't working*.
2. If we write *in pencil*, we can *rub out* what we write:
   I made notes in pencil at the side of the page, but rubbed them out before I took the book back to the library.
3. Note this expression:
   I think it's about time I put pen to paper and replied to that letter from my brother in Canada!
4. Another way of saying 'use a pen' is *write in ink*.
5. A *pen friend* or *pen pal* is someone you write to, but may never have met.
   When I was at school, I had a pen pal in France.
6. A *pen name* is a name used by a writer instead of his/her real name.

paper

Verb + paper	Adjective + paper	Noun + of + paper
cut paper	an examination paper	a bit / piece / scrap of paper
fold paper	recycled paper	a sheet of paper
tear paper	toilet paper	a pile of paper
	wrapping paper	both sides of the paper
	writing paper	

1. Verb and adjective collocations

Match the halves:

1. I must get some writing paper.
2. Make sure you write your name
3. Use a sharp pair of scissors
4. I need to buy some wrapping paper
5. Yoko made a paper hat
6. The book is made of very cheap paper
7. I always try to buy notebooks
8. We're out of toilet paper again.

a. for John's present.
b. which tears easily.
c. made of recycled paper.
d. Could you get some when you're out?
e. to cut the paper.
f. by folding a sheet of paper several times.
g. at the top of the examination paper.
h. It's time I wrote to Helen in Australia.

2. Noun + of + paper

Complete the sentences with the above nouns:

1. I wrote his phone number down on a . . . . of paper, but I've forgotten where I put it.
2. I thought I'd lost my keys, but I found them beneath a . . . . of paper on my desk.
3. Make sure you use a separate . . . . of paper for each question.
4. Please write on both . . . . of the paper.

form

Verb + form	Types of form
fill in / complete a form (in black ink)	an application form
sign a form	a consent form
date a form	an entry form
return a form	an order form

Expressions with form

Complete these sentences with one word:

1. This form must be . . . . by a parent before you can go on the school trip.
2. I . . . . in the form wrongly and had to do it again.
3. Make sure you sign and . . . . the form before sending it back to us.
4. Please complete the form and . . . . it to the school secretary by the end of the week.
5. I saw an advert for a job in last night's paper. I've sent off for an . . . . form.
6. All . . . . forms for the competition must be received by November 21.
7. Have the new books arrived yet? I filled in the . . . . form weeks ago.
8. Before my operation, the doctor asked me to sign a . . . . form.

Note   The form you fill in with details of your tax is called your *tax return*.

envelope and stamp

Expressions with envelope	**Verb + stamp**
open / close an envelope	buy a stamp
hand someone an envelope	lick a stamp
address an envelope	stick a stamp on the envelope
the envelope contains (money)	use a first-class / second-class stamp
write on the back of an envelope	collect stamps
a stamped addressed envelope (SAE)	

1. Expressions with envelope

Match the halves:

1. It's easier to open envelopes
2. The boss handed me an envelope which
3. Would you help me address these envelopes?
4. I had to enclose a stamped addressed envelope
5. I think I wrote Neil's phone number down

a. on the back of an old envelope.
b. with my letter of application.
c. contained my first week's wages.
d. There's a pen over there on the table.
e. with a paper knife.

2. Verb + stamp

Complete the sentences with the correct form of the above verbs:

1. . . . . a first-class stamp if you want the letter to get there tomorrow.
2. You can . . . . stamps in books of fives or tens from most newsagents.
3. I used to . . . . stamps when I was a child, but I lost interest when I went to high school.
4. I helped my mother with the Christmas cards by . . . . the stamps and . . . . them on the envelopes.

address

Verb + address	**Types of address**
write / print your address	your current address
send your address to (him)	your e-mail address
swap / exchange addresses	your full address
give me (your) address	your new address
get (their) address	a return address
lose (your) address	the above address
	(give) a false address

1. Verb + address

Complete the sentences with the correct form of the above verbs:

1. I can . . . . you the address of a good dentist if you ever need one.
2. Please . . . . your name and address in capital letters at the top of the paper.
3. Graham hasn't written to me for some time. Perhaps he's . . . . my address.
4. For further details, ... your name and address to BCR, PO Box 435, London.
5. Tell me. How did you . . . . my address?
6. We . . . . addresses with the people we met on holiday, and promised to send them some photographs when we got back home.

2. Types of address

Match the halves:

1.	Please write your full address	a.	on the 2nd of December.
2.	He gave a false name and address	b.	clearly on the form.
3.	I think Mark's e-mail address is	c.	his current address.
4.	Interviews will be held at the above address	d.	return address on the parcel.
5.	Once I've found somewhere to live, I'll send you	e.	on his business card.
6.	I didn't know who to send it back to. There was no	f.	to the police.
7.	The last address I have for him is in Boston. I don't know	g.	my new address.

Notes

1. Note these expressions:
   I'm afraid there's nobody called McDonald at this address.
   Please inform us of any change of address.
   I'll just take a note of your name and address. (write it down)

2. You write your *full address* or your *address in full.*

"We couldn't wait to open the parcel and see what was inside!"

parcel / package

> **Common expressions**
>
> send a parcel / package
> collect a parcel / package
> the parcel / package is addressed to (me)
> a parcel / package is waiting for you
>
> expect a parcel / package
> open a parcel / package
> weigh a parcel / package
> the parcel / package arrived / was delivered

Common expressions

Complete the sentences with the correct form of the above verbs:

1. Yes, I got the parcel. It was . . . . this morning around 7. Thanks very much.
2. It'll cost £8.50 to . . . . the parcel by airmail, or £2.50 by ordinary mail.
3. Alex, just a short message to say that there's a package . . . . for you at reception.
4. They'll need to . . . . the package at the post office to find out how much it'll cost.
5. The children were so excited that they . . . . the parcel as soon as it arrived.
6. You'll have to show some proof of identification when you go to . . . . the parcel.
7. I'm . . . . a parcel. Has anything arrived for me? The name's Dick, 12, Arbour St.
8. The package is . . . . to a Mr Eric Brown, but nobody of that name lives at this address.

Notes

1. Note these expressions:
   I called airport security after noticing a suspicious-looking package in the departure lounge.
   He sends regular food parcels to his family in Ethiopia.

2. We *wrap* or *tie up* parcels and packages:
   The parcel was wrapped in thick brown paper.
   Can you hold this parcel for me so I can tie it up?

Test 20

newspaper magazine pen pencil paper form envelope stamp address parcel / package

1. Identifying the key word

Choose the key word which collocates with these verbs, adjectives and nouns:

1. . . . .   break, sharpen, use, blunt
2. . . . .   read, subscribe to, write for, issue
3. . . . .   buy, lick, stick on, first-class
4. . . . .   read, glance at, local, copy
5. . . . .   hold, not work, write with, black
6. . . . .   address, open, write on
7. . . . .   cut, fold, tear, recycled
8. . . . .   collect, deliver, send, weigh
9. . . . .   fill in, sign, application, order
10. . . . .   exchange, print, full, e-mail

2. Choose the correct collocation

Choose the correct collocation:

1. Have you got *a copy / an issue* of today's newspaper I could borrow?
2. I *pay / subscribe to* a number of magazines, including Mojo and NME.
3. This pen's not *going / working*. Have you got a spare one you can lend me?
4. I need to sharpen my pencil. It's *blunt / short*.
5. Use a clean *page / sheet* of paper for each answer.
6. When you've finished filling *in / up* the form, hand it into the office.
7. Write your address in *full / whole* on the form.

3. Key word quiz

Complete each sentence with the correct key word:

1. Make sure you sign the application . . . . before you send it to us.
2. Can I borrow your sharpener? I've broken my . . . .
3. Write on both sides of the . . . .
4. It's a very colourful . . . ., aimed at young people between the ages of 15 and 18.
5. Don't forget to enclose a stamped addressed . . . . with your entry form.
6. I've lost his . . . ., but I've got his telephone number, if that's any help to you.
7. Please use a black . . . . to fill out the form.
8. I only had time to glance through the . . . . before I left for work.
9. Can you weigh this . . . . and tell me how much it will cost to send by airmail?
10. I hate licking . . . . It leaves a horrible taste in your mouth.

4. Prepositions

Choose the correct preposition to complete these expressions:

1. He works as a journalist *in / on* one of the local newspapers.
2. There's an interesting article *for / on* dieting in this magazine. Do you want to read it?
3. Please write *in / with* pencil. Don't use a pen.
4. Remember to stick a stamp *on / to* the envelope.
5. There's a parcel waiting *for / on* you at the post office.

Section 21

Work and entertainment

office

Common expressions

Complete the sentences with the correct form of the above verbs:

1. I . . . . in the company's busy Madrid office. It's air-conditioned and very comfortable.
2. I used to . . . . an office with Irene. She's now in another department.
3. I . . . . my wife's office three times this morning, but got no answer.
4. My husband works from home. He . . . . one of our bedrooms as an office.
5. The office I'm working in at the moment isn't very well . . . . – the manager is useless. That's why I'm looking for another job.
6. I usually try to . . . . the office before 7pm, so that I can get home in time to put the kids to bed.

Notes

1. Note these expressions:
   I got home exhausted after a hard day at the office.
   The atmosphere in our office is very relaxed / tense / friendly / formal.
2. Note the following expressions using *office + noun*:
   If you need a doctor, you have to call a different number outside normal office hours.
   I never listen to office gossip. It's usually nonsense!
   Our office party last Christmas was really excellent.
   I've just been promoted to office manager!

manager and secretary

Common expressions

Match the halves:

1. I asked to speak to the manager, but
2. Can you put me through
3. The manager sacked her because
4. I'll get my secretary
5. Liza has been promoted. She's become
6. If you are unable to come to work,
7. I'd complain to the manager
8. Michael works as a part-time secretary

a. she was often late for work.
b. the assistant manager of the York office.
c. she was in a meeting.
d. notify your line manager immediately.
e. to arrange a meeting for Thursday morning.
f. for a car hire company.
g. to the sales manager, please?
h. if you want something done about it.

factory

Common expressions

Complete the sentences with the correct form of the above verbs:

1. My dad works in a factory that . . . . car parts.
2. When you visit us, I'd be more than happy to . . . . you round our factory.
3. Many factories have been forced to . . . . down because of the poor economic situation in the country.
4. The factory will bring work to the area. It will . . . . about 400 new jobs.
5. Handel plc have just . . . . their first factory in the Far East.
7. I hate . . . . in factories – they're usually noisy places. I'd much rather work in an office.

employer, employee, (un)employment

Common expressions

Complete these sentences with one of the above words:

1. I live in an area of high . . . . It's almost impossible to find a job.
2. The new shoe factory will provide . . . . for hundreds of local people.
3. We will need a reference from your last . . . . before we interview you.
4. The shipyard has had to lay off about 100 . . . . because it has had no new orders.
5. Employer– . . . . relations have sunk to an all-time low. A strike is planned.
6. The unemployment . . . . is now at 15% and it's still rising!
7. I got a job as a secretary through an employment . . . .
8. Are you claiming unemployment . . . . while you're out of work?

Note | Note these expressions:
The National Health Service is the largest single employer in our town.
The government is determined to bring down unemployment.

police

Verb + police	Common expressions
call the police	police officer
the police arrest people	police station
the police investigate (murders)	police car
the police charge people with (murder)	police on the streets
the police search people for (guns)	report a crime to the police
the police warn people about (drugs)	the police carry guns
the police kill	the police offer rewards (for information)
the police are injured	the police appeal for witnesses to crimes

1. Verb + police

Complete the sentences with the correct form of the above verbs:

1. Police have . . . . two men in connection with last night's bank robbery in Exeter.
2. The police have . . . . Samuel Newton with the murder of his parents.
3. Police shot and . . . . three of the hijackers as they tried to escape from the plane.
4. The police . . . . me for drugs at the airport. I wonder why they stopped me!
5. Several police were badly . . . . during the demonstration, and were taken to hospital.
6. When I heard the explosion, I immediately picked up the phone and . . . . the police.
7. The police have . . . . people in the area around the prison to lock their doors at night.
8. Police are still . . . . the murder of the Harwich shopkeeper. They haven't found the murder weapon yet.

2. Common expressions

Match the halves:

1. Did you report
2. Police have offered a £1,000 reward
3. Police are appealing for witnesses
4. The British police do not normally
5. Crime will only go down
6. Two police cars overtook us,
7. I had to go to the police station
8. It took 6 police officers

a. when we have more police on the streets.
b. the theft of your bike to the police?
c. to identify the man I saw robbing the bank.
d. for information leading to the murderer's arrest.
e. to arrest the man.
f. to last night's fatal road accident.
g. carry guns.
h. lights flashing and sirens blaring.

Notes

1. Note these expressions:
   Police made 20 arrests at yesterday's demonstration.
2. The following expression means that the police think you committed the crime:
   A 35-year-old man is helping the police with their inquiries.
3. *Armed police* are police who are carrying guns, etc:
   Armed police quickly surrounded the bank.

soldier

Verb + soldier

Complete the sentences with the correct form of the above verbs:

1. One soldier was killed and three others were badly . . . . when their tank was hit by a rocket.
2. When the General came into the room, all the soldiers stood up and . . . .
3. Ten people were . . . . dead by soldiers during a demonstration in the capital yesterday.
4. Thousands of soldiers . . . . through the snow to their deaths.
5. The soldiers took no prisoners – they . . . . everyone in the village.

Now match the halves:

6. There's a monument in our village to all the soldiers
7. After a short battle, hundreds of enemy soldiers
8. At dawn US soldiers attacked the town
9. Soldiers who deserted in the First World War
10. Some soldiers think if they join the army,
11. The Queen was protected
12. The soldiers who lost their lives

a. died protecting our freedom.
b. who fought and died in the two World Wars.
c. from the crowd by about 20 soldiers.
d. were shot.
e. put down their guns and surrendered.
f. with tanks and helicopter gunships.
g. they'll see the world!

Notes
1. We say that a soldier *joins the army,* and then *serves in the army.* We also say that he *joins up.*
   Harry joined the army when he was 18.
2. Note the expression:
   The soldiers opened fire on the protestors. (started shooting at them).
3. When you have to join the army because of the law, we call it *conscription:*
   Many countries in Europe have abolished conscription.

museum / art gallery

Common expressions

Complete the sentences with one word:

1. I'm afraid the museum doesn't . . . . until 10 o'clock on Sundays.
2. Is there an entrance . . . . to get into the gallery?
3. I love . . . . art galleries and museums when I'm on holiday.
4. We hired a guide to . . . . us round the art gallery.
5. . . . . to the National Gallery is free.
6. The art gallery . . . . paintings by famous artists such as Picasso and Van Gogh.

Note   Note these expressions:
There's an exhibition of early photographs at the National Gallery of Modern Art this month.
There's a huge collection of old cars and buses on display at the Museum of Transport.
Please remember that photography is not permitted inside the art gallery.

cinema / theatre

Common expressions

Match the halves:

1. The new James Bond film is	a. at the National Theatre last week.
2. We saw a play by Shakespeare	b. It was only half full.
3. We're going to the cinema	c. can hold about 850 people.
4. There were plenty of seats in the cinema.	d. now showing at cinemas around the country.
5. The biggest theatre in town	e. to see the film, *Hours*. Do you want to come?
6. I managed to get us	f. ran for years and years at the Old Vic theatre.
7. The play *The Mousetrap*	g. the best seats in the theatre.

Notes   1. Note the expressions:
        What's on at the cinema / theatre tonight?

       2. A *multiplex cinema* is a place with several small cinemas in one building:
        There's a new multiplex cinema in our town with 20 screens.

       3. Note these different kinds of theatre:
        All the students were in the lecture theatre, but no lecturer arrived.
        The patient was taken to the operating theatre for an emergency operation.

show

Verb + show	Noun + preposition + show
enjoy a show	the opening night of a show
a show starts / finishes	a review of a show
a show is cancelled	the star of a show
a show is a success	a ticket for a show

1. Verb + show

Complete the sentences with the correct form of the above verbs:

1. We waited patiently in our seats for the show to . . . .
2. Just sit back and . . . . the show.
3. The show . . . . a spectacular success. Most of the critics loved it. It ran for two years.
4. They had to . . . . the show when four of the actors became ill.

2. Noun + preposition + show

Complete the sentences with the correct form of the above nouns:

1. I'd like two . . . . for the 5 o'clock show, please.
2. There's a really bad . . . . of the show in one of the Sunday papers.
3. This is the opening . . . . of our show, so many of us are feeling a little nervous.
4. For me, Larry Linslow was the . . . . of the show. He was brilliant as Captain Hook.

Note   Note that a show can be a type of television programme:
'Who Wants to Be a Millionaire' is a hugely popular TV show all over the world.
The pop star, Nick Cave, made a guest appearance on 'The Jools Holland Show'.
My grandmother seems to spend her days watching game shows on TV.

play, actor

Expressions with play	Expressions with actor
put on a play	become an actor
be in a play	actors bow (at the end of a show)
have a part in a play	a famous actor
write a play	a good / talented actor

Common expressions

Match the halves:

1. I've done a lot of acting.	a. become a famous actor one day.
2. Sam Desai has written plays	b. I've been in over 20 plays so far.
3. Many British primary schools put on	c. I had a small part in the school play last year.
4. Yes, I've acted once before.	d. and bowed at the end of the performance.
5. For me, Jack Nicholson is one of	e. for both television and the stage.
6. It's my dream to	f. the most talented actors I've ever seen.
7. All the actors came back onto the stage	g. a nativity play at Christmas time.

Note   A female actor used to be called *an actress*. Today many prefer to be called *actors*.

Test 21

1. Identifying the key word

Choose the key word which collocates with these verbs, adjectives and nouns:

1. . . . .   march, kill, salute, surrender
2. . . . .   famous, bow, talented
3. . . . .   call, share, work in, well-run
4. . . . .   arrest, call, officer, station
5. . . . .   open, shut down, visit, show around
6. . . . .   enjoy, review, star, ticket
7. . . . .   go to, half-full, packed
8. . . . .   be in, put on, write, part
9. . . . .   complain to, see, sacks people
10. . . . .   visit, entrance charge

2. The correct collocation

Choose the correct collocation:

1. I'm not very happy with the quality of this food. I'd like to *watch / see* the manager, please.
2. The factory *does / produces* most of the country's cars.
3. There's been *great / high* unemployment in the area since the local factory closed.
4. A number of soldiers were *hurt / wounded* in the attack.
5. There were no front *chairs / seats* left for the show. We had to sit at the back.
6. Let's go out and *see / look at* a film at the cinema tonight. I'm fed up watching videos at home.
7. Our local theatre group is putting *on / out* a play about poverty in Africa next week.
8. I'm appearing in the school play, but I only have a small *bit / part*.

3. Key word quiz

Complete each sentence with the correct key word:

1. A really nice guide showed us round the . . . .
2. The . . . . have arrested two men and charged them with murder.
3. When the general entered the room, all the . . . . saluted.
4. I love films with Jeremy Irons in them. He's my favourite . . . .
5. It's a large . . . . which can hold about 1000 people.
6. I work in a large . . . . on the fourth floor.
7. Before we can interview you for the job, we'll need a reference from your previous
. . . .
8. I hear you have tickets for the musical, *Cats and Dogs*. I hope you enjoy the . . . .

4. Prepositions

Choose the correct preposition to complete these expressions:

1. It's important that you report all crimes *at / to* the police.
2. I had a small part *in / on* the play.
3. I work *at / in* a large shoe factory.
4. There's no entrance charge *at / to* the museum.

Section 22

Technology and time

phone / telephone

Verb + phone	Phone + noun	Common expressions
answer the phone	a phone box	be on the phone
use the phone	a phone call	put the phone down on (him)
pick up / put down the phone	your phone number	the use of mobile phones
get off the phone	your phone bill	do something by phone
come to the phone	the telephone directory	speak to her on the phone
charge your mobile phone		leave the phone off the hook
the phone rings		your mobile phone

1. Verb +

Complete the sentences with the correct form of the above verbs:

1. I was just going to sleep when the phone . . . .
2. I've rung at least four times in the last hour. Nobody is . . . . the phone.
3. Do you mind if I . . . . your phone to make a quick call?
4. I forgot to . . . . my mobile phone last night, so that's why you couldn't reach me.

Complete the following two-part verbs with the correct preposition:

5. When I saw the smoke, I picked . . . . the phone and dialled 999.
6. I wish Shukri would get . . . . the phone. He's been . . . . it for hours!
7. It's a very bad line. Put the phone . . . . and I'll call you straight back.
8. I'm sorry he's too busy to come . . . . the phone. Shall I get him to call you back later?

2. Phone + noun

Complete the sentences with the correct form of the above nouns:

1. I'm sorry I don't have his phone . . . . or his address.
2. I'm sorry I wasn't able to return your phone . . . . earlier. I've been away from the office for a few days.
3. We tried looking up his number in the telephone . . . ., but it wasn't in the book.
4. We ran up a huge phone . . . . while we were away on holiday. I had no idea that international calls were that expensive!
5. I think that phone . . . . will soon be a thing of the past, now that nearly everybody has a . . . . phone.

3. Common expressions

Match the halves:

1. Who was that
2. Harry's number is still engaged.
3. The use of mobile phones is not permitted
4. The line's gone dead.
5. You can place your order

a. He's just put the phone down on me!
b. by phone or e-mail.
c. on the phone just now?
d. Maybe he's left the phone off the hook.
e. inside the aircraft.

Notes   1. Note the expression:
I read the exam results out to him over the phone.

2. Note the vocabulary we use specifically for mobile phones:
My new mobile phone has 50 ringtones.
I mostly use my mobile for texting.
Is your mobile pay-as-you-go?
My mobile needs re-charging.

call

"What's your number? I'll give you a call!"

1. Verb + call

Complete the sentences with the correct form of the above verbs:

1. I'll . . . . you a call this evening to see if you're feeling any better.
2. I . . . . a call from Keith last week. He's now in New Zealand.
3. Mr Harris isn't . . . . any calls just now. He's in a meeting.
4. It's cheaper to . . . . calls after 6pm. The rates are lower then.
5. Why haven't you . . . . any of my calls? I've phoned you at least three times and left a message each time.

2. Adjective + call

Match the halves:

1. The stolen painting was found
2. I don't make many long-distance calls,
3. There was no bomb in the building.
4. He was arrested for making
5. At the weekend
6. You'll have to ring me.

a. local calls are free.
b. The phone in my flat only accepts incoming calls.
c. so my phone bill is quite reasonable.
d. It was a hoax call.
e. after an anonymous call to a newspaper.
f. nuisance calls to single women.

Notes

1. Note these expressions:
   I was suddenly cut off in the middle of the call.
   Don't call us, we'll call you!
2. *Call* can also mean *visit*:
   It's time I paid a call on my Aunt Margaret. She lives alone and is always pleased to see me.
3. A *call centre* is where people work, dealing with customers on the phone.

camera

Common expressions

point the camera at (them)	look at the camera
smile at the camera	put a film in a camera
take the film out of a camera	act naturally in front of the camera
install security (CCTV) cameras	be caught on camera
a digital camera	a hidden camera

Common expressions

Complete these sentences with the correct form of the above verbs:

1. I'm having a problem getting a good picture of the baby. I can't get her to . . . . at the camera! She keeps looking away.
2. You always look so serious when you get your picture taken. Why don't you . . . . at the camera?
3. She . . . . her new digital camera at me, but I managed to put my hand up before she could take a picture.
4. The thief was arrested after he was . . . . on camera stealing CDs from the shop.
5. I just had time to . . . . the old film out of the camera and . . . . a new one in before the next race started.
6. My husband can't . . . . naturally in front of a camera. He always poses for his photograph.
7. The police say that crime in the city centre has decreased since CCTV cameras were . . . .

photograph / photo

Verb + photo

take photos
show photos to (you)
see a photo of (my family)
pose for a photo
get your photos developed
frame a photograph

Common expressions

carry a photo in your (wallet)
photos bring back memories
recognise someone from a photo
stick photos to a wall

1. Verb + photograph

Complete the sentences with the correct form of the above verbs:

1. Would you like to . . . . a photo of our new grandson in Canada? He's now 5 and our daughter sends us new photos of him every six months or so.
2. Did you . . . . many photographs while you were in China?
3. We all had to stand still and . . . . for a family photograph outside the church. There were almost 50 of us!
4. That's a great photo of you. You should get it . . . .
5. Pam brought some photographs of her family to school to . . . . the other students.
6. I need to get my holiday photos . . . . I can't wait to see what they look like! I just haven't had the time till now.

2. Common expressions:

Match the halves:

1. At the airport, I recognised Lars	a. some wonderful memories of my holiday there.
2. I carry a photo	b. Many of them were out of focus or too dark.
3. The photo of Goa brought back	c. from the photograph he had sent me.
4. The photos didn't come out very well.	d. his girlfriends all over his bedroom wall!
5. Kevin sticks photos of	e. of my wife in my wallet.

Notes

1. Note that we keep photos in an album:
   When was the last time you looked through your wedding album?
2. We often use *picture* to mean photo:
   Take a picture of me!
3. With a digital camera, you need to *download your photos onto your computer* and *print them at home*.
   With a conventional camera, you take the film to *a photo shop* and have it developed.
4. You can *enlarge a photo* you like and *have it framed*.

video / DVD

verb + video / DVD	**verb + video / DVD**
turn the video on	rent a video
stop the video	watch a video
work the video	make a video of (a wedding)
program the video	show a video
	The DVD of the film is out now.

1. Verb + video / DVD

Complete these sentences with the correct form of the above verbs:

1. I've . . . . the video to start recording *Neighbours* at 5 o'clock.
2. I don't know how to . . . . the video on. Do you?
3. Can you . . . . the video for a moment? I think I heard the doorbell.
4. Do you know how to . . . . the video recorder? I've no idea how to get it to start or eject a tape.

2. Verb + video / DVD

Match the halves:

1. I'm not sure how much	a. I think it comes out next month.
2. Let's stay at home tonight and watch a video.	b. to sell to raise money for charity.
3. Rewind the video to the beginning	c. I don't feel like going out.
4. They're making a video of the school play	d. before you return it to the video store.
5. The movie isn't out on DVD yet.	e. it costs to rent a video for a night.

Notes

1. A blank video is a cassette with nothing recorded on it:
   Has anyone got a blank video? I'd like to record the football while I'm out at work.
2. Video is being replaced by DVD these days:
   You can get the film on video or dvd.
3. Music is recorded on CD or cassette:
   The album is available on CD or cassette.
   They're giving away a free CD with this magazine.
   You've won the latest Coldplay CD plus two tickets for their concert in Glasgow.
   He downloads his favourite songs from the internet and burns them onto CDs.

minute, hour, week, month, year

<table>
<tr><td>

Verbs used with all key words

spend (a year in France)
take (a month to sail to South America)
last (a couple of hours)
wait (for 5 minutes)
waste (half an hour)

Key word + noun

a (30)-minute drive / walk / flight
a (5)-week waiting list
a (4)-year contract
a week's / month's notice

Key word + adjective / adverb

(5) minutes early / late
(6) months pregnant
(8) hours long
the (second) year running

</td><td>

Prepositional phrases

in a couple of minutes
for hours
during the week
at the end of the month
for the past year

(Number or amount) + a + key word

half an hour
(twice) a week
(£25) an hour
100 (cars) an hour
(40) hours a week

Common expressions

leave something to the last minute
enjoy every minute of (the show)
work long hours
be open 24 hours a day (24/7)
the summer / winter months
have a bad / good / busy week

</td></tr>
</table>

"The concert went on for hours, but we enjoyed every minute of it!"

1. Verb collocations:

Complete the sentences with the correct form of the above verbs:

1. Matthew, can I have a quick word? It won't . . . . a minute.
2. My son . . . . hours surfing the internet every day.
3. It's . . . . me a whole week to write this essay!
4. I had to . . . . weeks for my new passport to arrive!
5. If you take good care of your bike, it should . . . . for years.

2. Key word + noun

Match the halves:

1. My house is only a 5-minute
2. I think it's about a six-hour
3. I have to give at least two months'
4. There's now a six-month
5. Raul has signed a new three-year

a. waiting list for a heart by-pass operation.
b. contract with Real Madrid.
c. flight from London to New York.
d. walk from the school.
e. notice if I want to leave my job.

3. Key word + adjective / adverb

Complete the sentences with one of the above words:

1. Most films nowadays are about two hours . . . .
2. I was ten minutes . . . . for my interview because I missed my bus.
3. Manchester United have won the cup for the third year . . . .
4. My wife's about five months . . . . now.
5. We'd better have a coffee. We don't want to arrive a whole hour . . . . !

4. Prepositional phrases

Match the halves:

1. Hang on. I'll be ready	a. at the end of the month.
2. I was awake	b. for the past year.
3. I don't go out much	c. in a few minutes.
4. I've been out of work	d. during the week.
5. I get paid	e. for hours last night.

5. (Number / amount) + a + key word

Complete the sentences with the correct key word:

1. On average, I work about 35 hours a . . . .
2. The job's not that well-paid. I only get £4 an . . . .
3. I get my hair cut about once a . . . .
4. Edinburgh Castle attracts more than half a million tourists a . . . .
5. I waited for nearly 30 . . . . , but he didn't show up.

6. Common expressions

Match the halves:

1. The shop is very busy just now, so	a. to the last minute!
2. It's quite cold here in winter	b. I've had a bad week!
3. The supermarket is open	c. and enjoyed every minute of it.
4. Why do you always leave things	d. I'm working long hours – about 60 a week!
5. I went skiing for the first time last week	e. and very hot during the summer months.
6. Don't mention the office!	f. 24 hours a day.

Notes   1. Note that in all the sentences in exercise 5, except no 5, we can use 'per' in place of 'a / an':
He was driving at over 150 km per hour when the police stopped him.

2. Note these expressions:
That's the best news I've heard all week!
My kids get endless hours of fun from computer games.
I've just bought a new house, so I can't afford to go on holiday this year.

Test 22

1. Identifying the key word

Choose the key word which collocates with these verbs, adjectives and nouns:

1. . . . .   develop, frame, pose for, take
2. . . . .   programme, stop, turn on, work
3. . . . .   make, receive, local, hoax
4. . . . .   smile at, digital, CCTV
5. . . . .   answer, ring, use, number

2. The correct collocation

Choose the correct collocation:

1. The phone's ringing! Would someone *answer / make* it please?
2. I think I'll *give / make* Joanna a call. Have you got her number?
3. I'm not very good at *making / taking* photographs.
4. Do you have *a blank / an empty* video cassette? I want to record something tonight.
5. If you take good care of your camera, it should *keep / last* for years.
6. I *lost / wasted* over an hour trying to get through to the ticket office.
7. He *spends / takes* hours every day watching TV.
8. It only *takes / uses* about 20 minutes to learn how to use the machine.
9. I enjoyed *each / every* minute of the show.

3. Key word quiz

Complete each sentence with the correct key word:

1. I'm afraid I forgot to put a film in the . . . .!
2. Can you wait here while I go to the toilet? I won't be a . . . .
3. There's a new supermarket near us which opens 24 . . . . a day.
4. I wish she'd get off the . . . . I need to call Carlos.
5. I think I'll frame this . . . . and give it to my mother.
6. I'm sorry I forgot to return your . . . . I was very busy in the office.
7. Hang on! I won't be a . . . .!
8. Do you know how to turn on the . . . .?
9. Our team have won the competition for the third . . . . running.
10. Anne's about six . . . . pregnant now, so she'll be stopping work soon.

4. Common expressions with time

Complete these expressions with a suitable adjective or adverb:

1. Don't leave everything to the . . . . minute.
2. He works very . . . . hours. No wonder he's tired!
3. I've had a very . . . . week. I'll need to stay in bed all weekend to recover!
4. We arrived ten minutes . . . . , so we had time for a cup of coffee before the meeting.
5. Most films today are about two hours . . . .

answer key

Section 1
Your house

house 10
Ex 1: 1. shares 2. Moving 3. built 4. broke
5. renovating 6. demolished
Ex 2: 1-c 2-d 3-a 4-b

stairs 10
Ex 1: 1. use 2. running 3. fell 4. climb
Ex 2: 1-d 2-c 3-b 4-a

room 11
Ex 1: 1. tidy 2. share 3. lets
Ex 2: 1-c 2-d 3-h 4-e 5-a 6-f 7-b 8-g

floor 12
Ex 1: 1. swept 2. mopping 3. covered 4. scrubbed
Ex 2: 1-d 2-a 3-b 4-e 5-c

carpet 12
Ex 1: 1. lay 2. ruined 3. wear 4. hoover

wall 13
Ex 1: 1-g 2-a 3-e 4-b 5-f 6-d 7-h 8-c

ceiling 13
Ex 1: 1. touch 2. high 3. stared 4. hanging

door 14
Ex 1: 1. Close / Shut, slam 2. knock 3. break
4. lock
Ex 2: 1-d 2-c 3-a 4-e 5-b

light 14
Ex 1: 1-e 2-d 3-a 4-f 5-b 6-g 7-c

window 15
Ex 1: 1. break 2. cleaning 3. open 4. steam
Ex 2: 1-c 2-d 3-a 4-b

heating 15
Ex 1: 1. installed 2. broke, repair 3. have 4. turn
5. come 6. turn

Test 1 16
Ex 1: 1. room 2. window 3. door 4. floor
5. carpet 6. wall 7. ceiling 8. house
9. heating 10. stairs

Ex 2: 1. built 2. rented 3. sweep 4. climb
5. slam 6. see 7. switch off 8. vacuum
9. spare 10. top 11. high 12. thin
Ex 3: 1. room 2. floor or carpet 3. door 4. light
5. house 6. stairs 7. window 8. heating
Ex 4: 1. across 2. on 3. from 4. at

Section 2
Rooms and furniture

table 18
Ex 1: 1. lay / set 2. sits 3. clear 4. leave 5. get
6. shown 7. book
Ex 2: 1. at 2. round 3. across

drawer 18
Ex 1: 1. looked 2. top 3. stiff 4. back 5. opened
6. locks

chair 19
Ex 1: 1. back 2. from 3. off 4. back 5. in 6. into

mirror 19
Ex 1: 1-f 2-d 3-g 4-c 5-a 6-e 7-b

bed 20
Ex 1: 1. make 2. went 3. get 4. putting 5. change
Ex 2: 1. single 2. soft 3. comfortable 4. spare
5. bunk, bunk 6. unmade
Ex 3: 1-c 2-f 3-a 4-e 5-b 6-d

sheet, blanket, pillow, mattress, wardrobe,
alarm, curtains 21
Ex 1: 1. opened 2. extra 3. changes
4. set, go off / ring 5. clean 6. open 7. fitted
Ex 2: 1. in 2. on 3. with 4. into

bath and shower 22
Ex 1: 1. got 2. have 3. got 4. clean 5. bath
6. shower 7. bath 8. bath
Ex 2: 1. quick 2. long 3. cold 4. hot

towel 23
Ex 1: 1-f 2-d 3-e 4-g 5-a 6-c 7-b

toilet 23
Ex 1: 1. been 2. need 3. public 4. use 5. disabled
6. flush 7. ladies
Ex 2: 1. paper 2. seat 3. facilities

answer key

Ex 1: 1. chair 2. bed 3. alarm 4. table 5. mirror
6. toilet 7. drawer 8. towel 9. bath
10. shower

Ex 2: 1. lay 2. stiff 3. leaned 4. look 5. change
6. go 7. run 8. quick

Ex 3: 1. towel 2. bed 3. bath 4. table 5. blanket
6. drawer 7. wardrobe 8. windows 9. toilet
10. shower

Ex 4: 1. up 2. across 3. on 4. in 5. in

Section 3
In the kitchen

Ex 1: 1. left, turn 2. Turn 3. switch 4. empty
5. Put 6. take 7. put

Ex 2: 1. in 2. under 3. in(to) 4. from

Ex 3: 1-b 2-d 3-a 4-c

Ex 1: 1. Put 2. picked 3. holds

Ex 2: 1. blunt 2. serving 3. sharp 4. teaspoon

Ex 3: 1-d 2-c 3-a 4-b

Ex 1: 1. keep, locked 2. cleaning 3. filled 4. put
5. empty

Ex 1: 1. collapsed 2. put 3. put 4. top, get

Ex 1: 1. Fill 2. Cover 3. cleaning 4. Cook

Ex 2: 1-c 2-e 3-a 4-b 5-d

Ex 3: 1. teapot 2. chip pan 3. saucepan 4. frying
pan 5. soup pot 6. flower pot 7. coffee pot
8. cooking pots

Ex 1: 1. dropped, smashed 2. heaped 3. piled
4. cleared

Ex 2: 1-d 2-c 3-b 4-a

Ex 1: 1. filled 2. emptied 3. have 4. licking

Ex 1: 1. filled 2. put 3. poured 4. standing
5. use, blocked

Ex 1: 1-d 2-a 3-e 4-b 5-c

Ex 1: 1. Switch on 2. hold 3. stir 4. filled 5. put up
6. Cover 7. dinner 8. blocked 9. pile

Ex 2: 1. knife 2. cupboards 3. oven 4. pot
5. dishwasher 6. kettle 7. washing machine
8. pan 9. sink 10. fridge 11. dishes
12. cooker

Ex 3: 1. to 2. under 3. on 4. from 5. out of
6. from 7. in 8. down 9. with 10. in

Section 4
Sky and weather

Ex 1: 1-c 2-e 3-a 4-f 5-b 6-d

Ex 1: 1. came 2. rise / come up 3. avoid 4. go

Ex 2: 1-b 2-d 3-a 4-c

Ex 1: 1. disappeared 2. came 3. shining 4. come
5. see 6. appears

Ex 1: 1-c 2-d 3-a 4-b

Ex 1: 1. poured 2. got 3. holds 4. beat 5. spread
6. started

Ex 2: 1-c 2-a 3-b

Ex 3: 1. possibility 2. drops 3. break 4. shower
5. sound

Ex 4: 1. from 2. in 3. of 4. with

Ex 1: 1-b 2-c 3-d 4-a

answer key

cloud 37

Ex 1: 1. floating 2. covered 3. broke 4. lifted

Ex 2: 1. storm 2. white 3. low 4. thick

snow 38

Ex 1: 1. falling 2. clear 3. melt 4. drifted

Ex 2: 1-b 2-c 3-a

Ex 3: 1. falls 2. flakes 3. blanket

ice 38

Ex 1: 1. melted 2. skate 3. skidded 4. covered
5. slipped 6. crack 7. formed, scrape

wind 39

Ex 1: 1. changed, blow 2. drops / dies down
3. whistling 4. rise / get up 5. shelter
6. sailing

Ex 2: 1-c 2-d 3-a 4-b

fog 39

Ex 1: 1. lift / clear 2. lost 3. rolled

Test 4 40

Ex 1: 1. moon 2. rain 3. wind 4. cloud 5. sun
6. star 7. snow 8. fog 9. ice 10. sky

Ex 2: 1. cleared 2. avoid 3. full 4. shining 5. heavy
6. flashed 7. lifted 8. fall 9. forms 10. high

Ex 3: 1. sun 2. snow 3. wind 4. moon 5. rain
6. lightning 7. sky 8. ice 9. fog 10. stars

Ex 4: 1. under 2. behind 3. from 4. in

Section 5
The natural world

sea 42

Ex 1: 1. by 2. in 3. into 4. by 5. at

Ex 2: 1-b 2-a 3-d 4-c

wave 42

Ex 1: 1-c 2-f 3-e 4-b 5-d 6-a

river 43

Ex 1: 1. flow 2. froze 3. cross 4. pollute

Ex 2: 1. longest 2. wide 3. shallower

Ex 3: 1-c 2-f 3-a 4-e 5-d 6-b

island 44

Ex 1: 1. get 2. lived 3. leave 4. visiting 5. attracts
6. sailed

Ex 2: 1. remote 2. desert 3. tropical
4. uninhabited

beach 44

Ex 1: 1. lying 2. clean 3. going 4. stretched

Ex 2: 1-c 2-e 3-a 4-f 5-b 6-d

Ex 3: 1. along 2. to 3. at / on 4. on

sand 45

Ex 1: 1. getting 2. digging 3. buried 4. blew

Ex 2: 1-d 2-a 3-b 4-c

mountain 46

Ex 1: 1. highest 2. surrounded 3. climb 4. steep
5-b 6-c 7-d 8-a

Ex 2: 1. foot / bottom 2. side 3. view 4. top

forest 46

Ex 1: 1. destroyed 2. covered 3. cleared 4. path
5. shrunk 6. destruction

field 47

Ex 1: 1-d 2-a 3-b 4-c

ground 47

Ex 1: 1. to 2. on 3. above / off 4. below 5. to

Ex 2: 1-c 2-a 3-b

Test 5 48

Ex 1: 1. beach 2. mountain 3. island 4. sea 5. field
6. ground 7. wave 8. sand 9. forest 10. river

Ex 2: 1. rough 2. breaking 3. flows 4. attract
5. unspoilt 6. blows 7. highest 8. shrinking
9. plough

Ex 3: 1. beach 2. island 3. sea 4. mountain 5. field
6. wave 7. river 8. ground 9. sand

Ex 4: 1. at 2. by 3. through 4. on 5. against

Section 6
Animals and plants

animal 50

Ex 1: 1-d 2-f 3-e 4-a 5-c 6-b

bird and fish 50

Ex 1: 1. lay 2. built 3. catch 4. migrate 5. feed
6. swimming 7. flew

answer key

pet 51
Ex 1:   1. make 2. look 3. keep 4. feed

cat and dog 51
Ex 1:   1. looking 2. bitten 3. fed 4. attack 5. foul
6. barking
Ex 2:   1-d 2-a 3-e 4-b 5-c 6. feed 7. had
8. caught, purring 9. put 10. scratch

plant 52
Ex 1:   1. used 2. grows 3. produces 4. water
Ex 2:   1-b 2-c 3-a

crop 52
Ex 1:   1. ruined 2. spray 3. growing 4. plant,
harvest

flower 53
Ex 1:   1. grow 2. water 3. picked 4. arranging
5. send
Ex 2:   1. fresh 2. wild 3. artificial
Ex 3:   1-b 2-c 3-d 4-a

grass 53
Ex 1:   1. long, cut 2. Keep 3. lay

tree 54
Ex 1:   1. plant 2. climbing 3. grow 4. blown 5. cut
Ex 2:   1. off 2. with 3. into 4. under

garden 54
Ex 1:   1. working 2. tidy 3. digging 4. overgrown

fence 55
Ex 1:   1. climbs 2. put 3. mend
Ex 2:   1-d 2-c 3-a 4-b

gate 55
Ex 1:   1. school 2. left 3. shut 4. factory 5. garden

Test 6 56
Ex 1:   1. flower 2. cat 3. tree 4. animal 5. grass
6. bird 7. garden 8. dog 9. fence 10. plant
Ex 2:   1. treat 2. lay 3. make 4. bitten 5. had
6. produces 7. pick 8. fall off
Ex 3:   1. grass 2. pet 3. dog 4. bird 5. animals
6. flowers 7. garden 8. gate 9. cat 10. trees
Ex 4:   1. over 2. on 3. off 4. with 5. on 6. with

Section 7
Transport

car 58
Ex 1:   1. got 2. parked 3. drive 4. crashed
5. start 6. broke 7. skidded 8. hire
Ex 2:   1. economical 2. luxury 3. spacious
4. reliable 5. sports
Ex 3:   1. accidents 2. keys 3. alarm 4. park

bus 59
Ex 1:   1. missed 2. wait 3. stops 4. catch 5. get
6. leaves 7. run
Ex 2:   1. service 2. timetable 3. fare 4. stop

petrol 59
Ex 1:   1-c 2-e 3-a 4-f 5-b 6-d

plane 60
Ex 1:   1. caught 2. fly 3. boarded 4. land
5. crashed 6. delayed 7. diverted

airport 60
Ex 1:   1. closed 2. build 3. circle 4. from 5. at
6. to

train 61
Ex 1:   1. miss 2. change 3. catch 4. get 5. got
6-c 7-a 8-b
Ex 2:   1. to 2. in, in 3. on 4. by
Ex 3:   1-c 2-d 3-a 4-e 5-b

taxi 62
Ex 1:   1. drives 2. take 3. share 4. jumped 5. call
6. wait
Ex 2:   1. ride 2. driver 3. fare 4. rank

ferry 62
Ex 1:   1. cross 2. terminal 3. crossings 4. links /
connects 5. caught / took 6. board 7. sail

bike 63
Ex 1:   1. fell 2. get 3. ride 4. get 5. knocked
6. hire
Ex 2:   1-d 2-e 3-b 4-c 5-a

lorry 63
Ex 1:   1. drive 2. delivered 3. Loading
4. carrying 5. overturned

answer key

Ex 1: 1. bus /train 2. bike 3. ferry 4. car 5. lorry
6. train 7. taxi 8. airport 9. plane
10. petrol

Ex 2: 1. ride 2. get off 3. boarded 4. call 5. rank

Ex 3: 1. bike 2. ferry 3. bus 4. trains 5. car
6. lorry 7. plane 8. taxi 9. station

Ex 4: 1. on 2. by 3. out 4. into 5. at 6. along
7. in 8. at

Section 8
Travel

Ex 1: 1. Follow 2. cross 3. digging 4. blocked
5. build

Ex 2: 1. wrong 2. busy 3. clear 4. narrow 5. icy
6. main

Ex 3: 1. safety 2. signs 3. accidents

Ex 4: 1-b 2-a 3-f 4-g 5-d 6-c 7-e

Ex 1: 1. takes 2. make 3. complete 4. set 5. break

Ex 2: 1. safe 2. short 3. return 4. tiring 5. long
6. uneventful 7. awful

Ex 1: 1-c 2-a 3-d 4-b

Ex 2: 1. better / safer 2. Drunk 3. injured
4. learner

Ex 1: 1. lost 2. hold 3. endorsed 4. see

Ex 1: 1. robbed 2. visit 3. scared 4. arrive
5. attracted

Ex 2: 1-e 2-d 3-f 4-b 5-a 6-c

Ex 1: 1. day 2. coach 3. guided 4. Package

Ex 1: 1. lost 2. sold 3. buy, issue

Ex 2: 1. parking 2. plane 3. lottery 4. season

Ex 1: 1. join 2. standing 3. stretched 4. Are 5. jump

Ex 1: 1. reserve 2. Save 3. taken 4. gave 5. leave

Ex 2: 1. empty 2. back 3. aisle 4. good
5. uncomfortable 6. reclining

Ex 3: 1-d 2-c 3-b 4-a

Ex 1: 1. seat 2. licence 3. road 4. ticket 5. driver
6. tourist 7. journey 8. queue 9. tour

Ex 2: 1. clear 2. make 3. learner 4. clean
5. destination 6. stretched 7. taken

Ex 3: 1. driver 2. journey 3. tourists 4. ticket
5. licence 6. road 7. seat 8. queue 9. tour

Ex 4: 1. on 2. to 3. in 4. on 5. with 6. onto

Section 9
Meals and eating out

Ex 1: 1. skip 2. have 3. enormous 4. light,
continental, cooked 5. make

Ex 2: 1-d 2-a 3-b 4-c

Ex 1: 1. light 2. working 3. course 4. packed
5. Sunday 6. early

Ex 2: 1-b 2-a 3-d 4-c 5-f 6-e

Ex 1: 1. cooking / preparing 2. have 3. invite
4. coming

Ex 2: 1-d 2-e 3-b 4-a 5-c

Ex 1: 1. try 2. serves 3. working 4. recommend
5. runs

Ex 2: 1. expensive 2. Italian 3. cheap
4. fully booked

Ex 3: 1-b 2-c 3-a

Ex 1: 1-e 2-g 3-d 4-c 5-a 6-b 7-f

Ex 1: 1. have 2. paying 3. comes 4. split / divide
5. put

answer key

Ex 1:   1. meet 2. close 3. left
Ex 2:   1. at 2. behind 3. at 4. to
Ex 3:   1. licensed 2. crowded 3. Smoky 4. snack

Ex 1:   1-c 2-a 3-b

Ex 1:   1. ordered 2. handed 3. have / get
        4. includes 5. study 6. finished 7. share
        8. children's

Ex 1:   1. book 2. one 3. free 4. ready
        5. non-smoking 6. by

Ex 1:   1. restaurant 2. bill 3. waiter / waitress
        4. dinner / lunch 5. breakfast 6. menu
        7. lunch 8. service 9. table 10. bar
Ex 2:   1. skip 2. light 3. invite 4. serves 5. call
        6. comes to 7. study 8. ready
Ex 3:   1. lunch 2. waiter 3. dinner 4. bar 5. menu
        6. table, restaurant 7. breakfast 8. bill
        9. service
Ex 4:   1. over 2. for 3. of 4. behind 5. by 6. on

Section 10
Drink

Ex 1:   1. drinking 2. poured 3. spilt 4. have
        5. make
Ex 2:   1. hot 2. fresh 3. white 4. quick 5. strong
        6. instant
Ex 3:   1-b 2-e 3-d 4-c 5-a

Ex 1:   1. make 2. served 3. have 4. brought
        5. drank
Ex 2:   1. iced 2. weak 3. sweet 4. hot
Ex 3:   1-d 2-a 3-b 4-c

Ex 1:   1. brews 2. ordered 3. Have 4. drink
Ex 2:   1. low-alcohol 2. cool / cold 3. flat
        4. draught

Ex 3:   1-d 2-a 3-b 4-c

Ex 1:   1. drink 2. spilt 3. store 4. served
        5. poured
Ex 2:   1. dry 2. sparkling 3. best / finest 4. white
        5. cheap
Ex 3:   1-b 2-a 3-e 4-c 5-d

Ex 1:   1. drank 2. open 3. recycle 4. passed
        5. plastic 6. shake 7. full, empty
Ex 2:   1. off 2. on 3. of 4. back

Ex 1:   1. knocked 2. smashed 3. held 4. filled
        5. raise
Ex 2:   1-e 2-a 3-b 4-d 5-c

Ex 1:   1. hold 2. filled 3. prefer 4. knocked
        5. handed 6. picked
Ex 2:   1. half 2. chipped 3. plastic 4. dirty

Ex 1:   1. bottle 2. wine 3. coffee 4. cup 5. tea
        6. glass 7. beer
Ex 2:   1. make 2. weak 3. draught 4. unscrew
        5. over 6. iced 7. strong
Ex 3:   1. wine 2. bottles 3. coffee 4. beer 5. glass
        6. tea 7. cups
Ex 4:   1. jar 2. pot 3. pack 4. case 5. pint
Ex 5:   1. quick 2. label 3. cracked 4. sparkling
        5. mug

Section 11
Shopping and food 1

Ex 1:   1. running 2. sells 3. go (down) 4. opens
        5. leave 6. works 7. broke
Ex 2:   1-d 2-f 3-e 4-a 5-c 6-b
Ex 3:   1. from 2. in 3. to 4. around 5. in

Ex 1:   1. need 2. shop 3. open 4. stop 5. stacking

Ex 1:   1-d 2-e 3-f 4-a 5-c 6-b

answer key

meat 92
Ex 1: 1. cooked 2. eat 3. Fry 4. gone 5. slice 6. Chop
Ex 2: 1-c 2-d 3-a 4-e 5-f 6-b

chicken 92
Ex 1: 1-f 2-d 3-e 4-b 5-c 6-a

fish 93
Ex 1: 1-c 2-e 3-f 4-a 5-b 6-d

oil 93
Ex 1: 1. Fry 2. Heat 3. Add 4. Pour

egg 93
Ex 1: 1-g 2-d 3-b 4-c 5-f 6-e 7-a

milk 94
Ex 1: 1. poured 2. take 3. comes / came 4. heat
       5. used
Ex 2: 1-b 2-d 3-e 4-a 5-c

cheese 94
Ex 1: 1-f 2-e 3-d 4-c 5-b 6-a

vegetables 95
Ex 1: 1. steam 2. grow 3. store 4. overcooked
Ex 2: 1-d 2-c 3-b 4-a

fruit 95
Ex 1: 1. peeled 2. wash 3. rot 4. picking
Ex 2: 1-d 2-c 3-b 4-a

Test 11 96
Ex 1: 1. fish 2. chicken 3. supermarket
       4. customer 5. cheese 6. milk 7. oil 8. fruit
       9. egg 10. meat 11. shop 12. vegetable
Ex 2: 1. off 2. regular 3. tender 4. Heat 5. take
       6. fresh
Ex 3: 1. supermarket 2. meat 3. fish 4. fruit 5. oil
       6. customers 7. milk 8. egg 9. cheese
       10. shop
Ex 4: 1. in 2. into 3. to 4. around

Section 12
Food 2

bread 98
Ex 1: 1-c 2-f 3-b 4-e 5-d 6-a
Ex 2: 1. smell 2. slices 3. chunks 4. loaf

sandwich 98
Ex 1: 1. ordered 2. have 3. serve 4. made

cake and biscuit 99
Ex 1: 1. eaten 2. baking / making 3. try 4. cut
Ex 2: 1. birthday 2. slice 3. home-made 4. recipe
       5. chocolate
Ex 3: 1-e 2-d 3-a 4-b 5-c

pasta 100
Ex 1: 1. cook 2. boil 3. eat 4. drain
Ex 2: 1-c 2-d 3-a 4-b

rice 100
Ex 1: 1-g 2-e 3-d 4-c 5-b 6-a 7-f

potatoes 101
Ex 1: 1. boil 2. peeling 3. slice 4. grow

chips 101
Ex 1: 1-d 2-c 3-b 4-a

chocolate 102
Ex 1: 1. melted 2. plain 3. broke 4. addicted, bars,
       like 5. box

sugar 102
Ex 1: 1. take / have 2. contains 3. sprinkle 4. put
Ex 2: 1-f 2-c 3-d 4-b 5-e 6-a

salt 103
Ex 1: 1. pass 2. add 3. sprinkle 4. cut
Ex 2: 1-e 2-c 3-d 4-b 5-a

Test 12 104
Ex 1: 1. potatoes 2. bread 3. salt 4. biscuit
       5. cake 6. chocolate 7. rice 8. sandwich
       9. sugar 10. pasta 11. chips
Ex 2: 1. spread 2. make 3. baked 4. peel 5. dark
Ex 3: 1. sandwich 2. chips 3. biscuits 4. bread
       5. rice, rice 6. cake 7. salt 8. pasta
Ex 4: 1. loaf 2. recipe 3. slice 4. packet
       5. bowl / helping / plate 6. grains
       7. portions 8. bar 9. sachets 10. pinch

answer key

Section 13
Your body

body 106
Ex 1:   1-h 2-d 3-b 4-c 5-g 6-e 7-f 8-a

muscle 106
Ex 1:   1. tense 2. build up 3. pulled 4. massage
        5. feel 6. soothe

skin 107
Ex 1:   1-f 2-c 3-b 4-e 5-d 6-a

stomach 107
Ex 1:   1. rumbling 2. upset 3. lying 4. holding
Ex 2:   1-f 2-c 3-b 4-e 5-d 6-a

waist and back 108
Ex 1:   1. put 2. wrapped 3. reaches 4. strip
Ex 2:   1-d 2-c 3-e 4-a 5-b

arm 108
Ex 1:   1. stiff 2. long 3. broke 4. aching 5. broken
        6. folded
Ex 2:   1. under 2. round 3. in 4. into

wrist 109
Ex 1:   1. cutting 2. sprained 3. held 4. broke

leg 109
Ex 1:   1. broke 2. lost 3. shave 4. rubbing
        5. amputate
Ex 2:   1-c 2-e 3-d 4-a 5-b

finger 110
Ex 1:   1-e 2-f 3-g 4-b 5-a 6-d 7-c

nail and toe 110
Ex 1:   1. broken 2. cut 3. painting 4. grow, bite
Ex 2:   1. stand 2. touch 3. step 4. covered

knee 111
Ex 1:   1. hurt, need 2. bend 3. came 4. got
        5. scraped / grazed

foot 111
Ex 1:   1. wash 2. Lift 3. standing 4. wipe
Ex 2:   1. bare 2. freezing 3. smelly 4. dirty
Ex 3:   1-d 2-c 3-a 4-b

Test 13 112
Ex 1:   1. skin 2. nail 3. stomach 4. arm 5. knee
        6. finger 7. back 8. feet 9. muscle 10. waist
        11. body 12. leg 13. toe 14. wrist
Ex 2:   1. aching 2. pulled 3. upset 4. hurt
Ex 3:   1. leg 2. skin 3. feet 4. arms 5. stomach
        6. toes, knees 7. fingers 8. back 9. muscles
        10. waist
Ex 4:   1. at 2. under 3. on 4. round 5. in 6. on

Section 14
Head and shoulders

hair 114
Ex 1:   1. wash 2. brush 3. dye 4. cut, cuts 5. losing
Ex 2:   1. curly 2. grey 3. dry 4. fair 5. wet
        6. short

beard and moustache 114
Ex 1:   1. had 2. grow 3. trim 4. shave

face 115
Ex 1:   1. forgets 2. wiping 3. wash 4. splashed
Ex 2:   1-d 2-c 3-a 4-b
Ex 3:   1. to 2. on 3. in / with 4. to 5. in 6. down

mouth 116
Ex 1:   1. close 2. open 3. wiped 4. burnt
Ex 2:   1-d 2-a 3-b 4-c

tooth 116
Ex 1:   1. broke 2. brushing 3. lost 4. taken
Ex 2:   1-c 2-d 3-b 4-a

tongue, lips, kiss, smile 117
Ex 1:   1. burnt 2. had 3. licked 4. stuck 5. lifted
        6. bit
Ex 2:   1. big 2. friendly 3. goodnight 4. dry
        5. lovely 6. first

throat 117
Ex 1:   1-b 2-e 3-d 4-c 5-a

ear 118
Ex 1:   1. has 2. stick 3. pierced 4. whispered
        5. put

answer key

nose 118
Ex 1:   1. hold 2. blew 3. picked 4. bleeding
        5. blocked 6. running 7. broke 8. wiping

neck 119
Ex 1:   1-c 2-d 3-b 4-a

shoulder 119
Ex 1:   1. dislocated 2. has 3. massage 4. looking
        5. shrugged
Ex 2:   1. round 2. off 3. on 4. over 5. on 6. onto

Test 14 120
Ex 1:   1. face 2. nose 3. hair 4. throat 5. teeth
        6. mouth 7. beard / moustache 8. lips 9. ear
        10. smile 11. shoulder 12. neck 13. tongue
        14. kiss
Ex 2:   1. dyed 2. out 3. wipe 4. a sore 5. blow
        6. shrugged
Ex 3:   1. face 2. teeth 3. neck 4. beard 5. throat
        6. lips 7. hair 8. tongue
Ex 4:   1. in 2. round 3. on 4. over 5. in

Section 15
Clothes

trousers 122
Ex 1:   1. iron 2. Try 3. take 4. pulled 5. wearing
Ex 2:   1-e 2-f 3-d 4-c 5-a 6-b

shirt 122
Ex 1:   1-c 2-e 3-a 4-f 5-b 6-d

tie 123
Ex 1:   1. loosened 2. wearing 3. black 4. school
        5. put 6. tie 7. plain

sweater 123
Ex 1:   1. washed 2. knitting 3. wearing 4. shrunk
        5. put
Ex 2:   1-c 2-d 3-a 4-b

dress 124
Ex 1:   1. wearing 2. fit 3. fastens 4. try 5. made
Ex 2:   1-e 2-d 3-b 4-f 5-a 6-c

coat 124
Ex 1:   1. put 2. wearing 3. Hang 4. Take

Ex 2:   1. winter 2. Fur 3. long

hat 125
Ex 1:   1. tried 2. wearing 3. put 4. hold 5. take

uniform 125
Ex 1:   1-f 2-a 3-d 4-e 5-b 6-c

scarf and gloves 126
Ex 1:   1-d 2-e 3-f 4-a 5-c 6-b

sock 126
Ex 1:   1. put 2. wear 3. changed
Ex 2:   1-d 2-e 3-a 4-c 5-b

shoe 127
Ex 1:   1. try 2. wearing 3. polished 4. took
Ex 2:   1-f 2-c 3-a 4-e 5-d 6-b

Test 15 128
Ex 1:   1. shoe 2. glove 3. sweater / scarf 4. scarf
        5. uniform 6. sock 7. shirt 8. hat 9. dress
        10. tie 11. coat 12. trousers
Ex 2:   1. sleeves 2. matches 3. fastens 4. fit
Ex 3:   1. shirts 2. coat 3. tie 4. hat 5. socks
        6. sweater 7. shoes 8. trousers 9. scarf
        10. dress 11. gloves 12. uniform
Ex 4:   1. on 2. on 3. over 4. with 5. in

Section 16
Personal items

pocket 130
Ex 1:   1. searched 2. empty 3. hole 4. go 5. back
        6. inside

belt, button, zip 130
Ex 1:   1. do 2. belt 3. buttons 4. belt 5. came
        6. fasten 7. unbuckled 8. buttons

bag 131
Ex 1:   1. lift 2. carry 3. dropped 4. fill 5. emptied
Ex 2:   1-d 2-f 3-e 4-a 5-g 6-b 7-c
Ex 3:   1. mix-up 2. check 3. astray 4. searched

wallet 132
Ex 1:   1. left 2. stolen 3. carry 4. took 5. forgot
        6. put

answer key

card 132
Ex 1:   1. credit, debit, credit, debit   2. phone
        3. business   4. identity   5. donor

key 133
Ex 1:   1. find   2. put   3. hand in   4. cut   5. hidden
        6. lost   7. mislaid
Ex 2:   1-d   2-c   3-e   4-a   5-b

ring 133
Ex 1:   1. belonged   2. wear   3. show   4. valued   5. fit

glasses 134
Ex 1:   1. put   2. wearing   3. broke   4. took   5. have
        6. need
Ex 2:   1-e   2-d   3-b   4-c   5-a

lenses 134
Ex 1:   1. soft   2. coloured   3. solution   4. daily-wear
        5. soak, wearing

umbrella 135
Ex 1:   1. put   2. lost   3. bring   4. take   5. hold
        6. forgot   7. put

watch 135
Ex 1:   1. glanced / looked   2. stopped   3. wear   4. put
        5. set
Ex 2:   1-d   2-e   3-b   4-a   5-c

Test 16 136
Ex 1:   1. bag   2. umbrella   3. button   4. wallet
        5. ring   6. glasses   7. key   8. pocket   9. card
        10. lenses   11. watch   12. belt   13. zip
Ex 2:   1. bunch   2. slow   3. thick
Ex 3:   1. belt   2. ring   3. bag   4. pockets   5. glasses
        6. watch   7. keys   8. button   9. lenses
        10. umbrella   11. zip   12. card   13. wallet
Ex 4:   1. by   2. with   3. at   4. under   5. to

Section 17
The family

parent 138
Ex 1:   1. divorced   2. met   3. worry   4. please
        5. brought
Ex 2:   1-c   2-a   3-d   4-b
Ex 3:   1. strict   2. elderly   3. single   4. working
        5. foster

child / children 139
Ex 1:   1. looks   2. bring   3. playing   4. teased
        5. neglect   6. taught   7. adopted, have
Ex 2:   1. only   2. grown-up   3. small / young
        4. average   5. gifted   6. spoilt   7. well-behaved
Ex 3:   1-c   2-a   3-d   4-b

wedding 140
Ex 1:   1. invited   2. pay   3. going   4. have   5. held
        6. called
Ex 2:   1. speech   2. Congratulations   3. guests
        4. video
Ex 3:   1-e   2-f   3-d   4-g   5-a   6-b   7-c

husband, wife 141
Ex 1:   1. lives   2. lost   3. left   4. met   5. looking
Ex 2:   1. present   2. loving   3. former / ex-   4. late

funeral 141
Ex 1:   1. held, service   2. wear   3. arrange
        4. attended   5. cremation

baby 142
Ex 1:   1. had   2. expecting   3. look   4. held   5. wake
        6. calling   7. feed
Ex 2:   1. crying   2. weighed   3. playing   4. due
        5. born   6. sleeping

birth 142
Ex 1:   1-c   2-d   3-e   4-b   5-f   6-a

birthday 143
Ex 1:   1. having   2. getting   3. celebrate   4. forgot
        5. wishes
Ex 2:   1. cake   2. present   3. card   4. party

present 143
Ex 1:   1. get   2. unwraps   3. thank   4. buying
        5. wrapped
Ex 2:   1-c   2-a   3-d   4-b

Test 17 144
Ex 1:   1. baby   2. birthday   3. birth   4. parent
        5. wedding   6. funeral   7. present   8. child /
        children   9. husband / wife
Ex 2:   1. a single   2. an only   3. quiet   4. former
        5. had   6. gave   7. leaving   8. lovely

answer key

Ex 3: 1. birthday 2. children 3. birth 4. wedding
5. present 6. funeral 7. baby 8. husband
9. parents
Ex 4: 1. as 2. at 3. in 4. on 5. you

Section 18
Health and sport

hospital 146
Ex 1: 1. going 2. kept 3. treated 4. come 5. at
6. with 7. by 8. in

doctor 146
Ex 1: 1. call 2. prescribed 3. see 4. consult
5. referred 6. examined

headache, cough, cold, virus 147
Ex 1: 1. gone 2. given 3. had 4. relieving
5. complaining
Ex 2: 1-d 2-a 3-e 4-c 5-b
Ex 3: 1. have 2. caught 3. clear 4. shake
Ex 4: 1. going 2. causes 3. picked

medicine, pill 148
Ex 1: 1. give 2. keep 3. taking 4. made 5. tastes
6. take
Ex 2: 1-e 2-a 3-d 4-c 5-b

injection 148
Ex 1: 1. gave 2. hurt 3. having 4. needed / had

blood 149
Ex 1: 1-h 2-a 3-e 4-f 5-c 6-d 7-b 8-g

bandage, stitches, x-ray 149
Ex 1: 1. needed 2. removed 3. have 4. put
5. showed 6. get 7. have

ball 150
Ex 1: 1. bounced 2. playing 3. rolled 4. missed
5. catch, throw

football 150
Ex 1: 1-c 2-d 3-e 4-b 5-a
Ex 2: 1. team 2. match 3. player 4. pitch 5. fans
6. strip, boots

score, result 151
Ex 1: 1-b 2-c 3-a 4-e 5-d

player 151
Ex 1: 1. signing 2. beaten 3. scored 4. signed
5. warming 6. earn
Ex 2: 1. greatest 2. competitive 3. experienced
4. exciting

Test 18 152
Ex 1: 1. cold 2. doctor 3. injection 4. cough
5. hospital 6. bandage 7. medicine 8. virus
9. x-ray 10. pill 11. headache 12. stitches
13. blood 14. football 15. result 16. score
17. ball 18. player
Ex 2: 1. doctor 2. blood 3. headache 4. medicine
5. stitches 6. hospital 7. cough 8. pills
9. x-ray 10. cold 11. injection 12. virus
13. bandage 14. ball 15. result 16. score
17. players 18. football

Section 19
Education

school 154
Ex 1: 1. left 2. start 3. missed 4. collect 5. change
6. expelled 7. playing 8. attend, went
Ex 2: 1-d 2-e 3-g 4-a 5-b 6-c 7-f
Ex 3: 1. for 2. at 3. through 4. from 5. after

teacher 155
Ex 1: 1. corrects 2. returned 3. told 4. become
5. taught 6. punish
Ex 2: 1-d 2-e 3-g 4-a 5-f 6-b 7-c

student 156
Ex 1: 1. taught 2. bullied 3. graduate, drop
Ex 2: 1. bright / brilliant 2. angry 3. fellow
4. former 5. full-time 6. lazy
Ex 3: 1-b 2-a 3-e 4-c 5-d

class and lesson 157
Ex 1: 1-e 2-f 3-d 4-c 5-b 6-a
Ex 2: 1. enjoy 2. give 3. spent 4. going 5. had
6. preparing

answer key

test 157
Ex 1:   1. cheats 2. pass 3. revise 4. marking
        5. do / sit / take

book 158
Ex 1:   1. written 2. closed 3. finishing 4. reading
        5. enjoyed
Ex 2:   1. longest 2. good 3. boring 4. interesting
        5. heavy-going
Ex 3:   1. chapter 2. title 3. author 4. pile 5. copy
        6. pages
Ex 4:   1-d 2-c 3-a 4-b

page 159
Ex 1:   1-c 2-a 3-d 4-b
Ex 2:   1. front 2. blank 3. new 4. opposite
Ex 3:   1. on 2. at 3. to 4. on 5. over 6. of

Test 19 160
Ex 1:   1. page 2. class 3. school 4. test 5. student
        6. lesson 7. teacher 8. book
Ex 2:   1. expelled 2. become 3. out 4. missed
        5. gave 6. did 7. title 8. blank
Ex 3:   1. student 2. lessons 3. test 4. pages
        5. teacher 6. class 7. lesson 8. school
Ex 4:   1. for 2. to 3. on 4. in 5. through 6. on

Section 20
Reading and writing

newspaper 162
Ex 1:   1. recycle 2. glance 3. buying, read
        4. reported
Ex 2:   1. with 2. to 3. in 4. on
Ex 3:   1-c 2-e 3-a 4-b 5-d

magazine 163
Ex 1:   1. bought, read 2. aimed 3. published
        4. write 5. subscribe
Ex 2:   1. range 2. page 3. editor 4. issue
        5. readers
Ex 3:   1-c 2-e 3-a 4-b 5-d

pen and pencil 164
Ex 1:   1-f 2-d 3-g 4-b 5-a 6-c 7-e
Ex 2:   1. broke 2. sharpen, sharpener 3. wrote
        4. blunt, sharp 5. use 6. draw

paper 165
Ex 1:   1-h 2-g 3-e 4-a 5-f 6-b 7-c 8-d
Ex 2:   1. bit / piece / scrap 2. pile 3. sheet 4. sides

form 165
Ex 1:   1. signed 2. filled 3. date 4. return
        5. application 6. entry 7. order 8. consent

envelope and stamp 166
Ex 1:   1-e 2-c 3-d 4-b 5-a
Ex 2:   1. Use 2. buy 3. collect 4. licking, sticking

address 166
Ex 1:   1. give 2. write 3. lost 4. send 5. get
        6. swapped / exchanged
Ex 2:   1-b 2-f 3-e 4-a 5-g 6-d 7-c

parcel / package 167
Ex 1:   1. delivered 2. send 3. waiting 4. weigh
        5. opened 6. collect 7. expecting
        8. addressed

Test 20 168
Ex 1:   1. pencil 2. magazine 3. stamp 4. newspaper
        5. pen 6. envelope 7. paper 8. package /
        parcel 9. form 10. address
Ex 2:   1. a copy 2. subscribe to 3. working 4. blunt
        5. sheet 6. in 7. full
Ex 3:   1. form 2. pencil 3. paper 4. magazine
        5. envelope 6. address 7. pen 8. newspaper
        9. parcel / package 10. stamps
Ex 4:   1. on 2. on 3. in 4. on 5. for

Section 21
Work and entertainment

office 170
Ex 1:   1. work 2. share 3. called 4. uses 5. run
        6. leave

manager and secretary 170
Ex 1:   1-c 2-g 3-a 4-e 5-b 6-d 7-h 8-f

factory 171
Ex 1:   1. makes / produces 2. show 3. shut / close
        4. create 5. set up / opened 6. working

answer key

employer, employee, (un)employment . . 171

Ex 1: 1. unemployment 2. employment
3. employer 4. employees 5. employee
6. rate 7. agency 8. benefit

police 172

Ex 1: 1. arrested 2. charged 3. killed 4. searched
5. injured 6. called 7. warned 8. investigating
Ex 2: 1-b 2-d 3-f 4-g 5-a 6-h 7-c 8-e

soldier 173

Ex 1: 1. wounded 2. saluted 3. shot 4. marched
5. killed 6-b 7-e 8-f 9-d 10-g 11-c
12-a

museum / art gallery 174

Ex 1: 1. open 2. charge 3. visiting 4. show
5. Entrance 6. contains

cinema / theatre 174

Ex 1: 1-d 2-a 3-e 4-b 5-c 6-g 7-f

show 175

Ex 1: 1. start 2. enjoy 3. was 4. cancel
Ex 2: 1. tickets 2. review 3. night 4. star

play, actor 175

Ex 1: 1-b 2-e 3-g 4-c 5-f 6-a 7-d

Test 21 176

Ex 1: 1. soldier 2. actor 3. office 4. police
5. factory 6. show 7. cinema / theatre
8. play 9. manager 10. museum / art gallery
Ex 2: 1. see 2. produces 3. high 4. wounded
5. seats 6. see 7. on 8. part
Ex 3: 1. museum / art gallery 2. police 3. soldiers
4. actor 5. cinema / theatre 6. office
7. employer 8. show
Ex 4: 1. to 2. in 3. in 4. to

Section 22
Technology and time

phone / telephone 178

Ex 1: 1. rang 2. answering 3. use 4. charge 5. up
6. off, on 7. down 8. to
Ex 2: 1. number 2. call 3. directory 4. bill
5. boxes, mobile
Ex 3: 1-c 2-d 3-e 4-a 5-b

call 179

Ex 1: 1. give 2. got / received 3. taking 4. make
5. returned
Ex 2: 1-e 2-c 3-d 4-f 5-a 6-b

camera 180

Ex 1: 1. look 2. smile 3. pointed 4. caught
5. take, put 6. act 7. installed

photograph / photo 180

Ex 1: 1. see 2. take 3. pose 4. framed 5. show
6. developed
Ex 2: 1-c 2-e 3-a 4-b 5-d

video / DVD 181

Ex 1: 1. programmed 2. turn 3. stop 4. work
Ex 2: 1-e 2-c 3-d 4-b 5-a

minute, hour, week, month, year 182

Ex 1: 1. take 2. spends 3. taken 4. wait 5. last
Ex 2: 1-d 2-c 3-e 4-a 5-b
Ex 3: 1. long 2. late 3. running 4. pregnant
5. early
Ex 4: 1-c 2-e 3-d 4-b 5-a
Ex 5: 1. week 2. hour 3. month 4. year
5. minutes
Ex 6: 1-d 2-e 3-f 4-a 5-c 6-b

Test 22 184

Ex 1: 1. photograph 2. video / DVD 3. call
4. camera 5. phone / telephone
Ex 2: 1. answer 2. give 3. taking 4. a blank 5. last
6. wasted 7. spends 8. takes 9. every
Ex 3: 1. camera 2. minute 3. hours 4. phone
5. photograph 6. call 7. minute 8. video /
DVD 9. year 10. months
Ex 4: 1. last 2. long 3. busy 4. early 5. long

alphabetical list of words

actor	**175**	chips	101	form	165
address	166	chocolate	102	freezer	26
airport	60	cinema	174	fridge	26
alarm	21	class	157	fruit	95
animal	50	cloud	37	funeral	141
arm	108	coffee	82		
art gallery	174	coat	124	**garden**	**54**
		cold	147	gate	55
baby	**142**	cooker	26	glass	86
back	108	cough	147	glasses	134
bag	131	crop	52	gloves	126
ball	150	cup	87	grass	53
bandage	149	cupboard	28	grill	26
bar	78	curtains	21	ground	47
bath	22	customer	91		
beach	44			**hat**	**125**
beard	114	**dinner**	**75**	hair	114
beer	84	dishes	31	headache	147
bed	20	dishwasher	26	heating	15
belt	130	dog	51	hospital	146
bike	63	doctor	146	hour	182
bill	77	door	14	house	10
bird	50	drawer	18	husband	141
birth	142	dress	124		
birthday	143	driver	68	**ice**	**38**
biscuit	99	DVD	181	injection	148
blanket	21			island	44
blood	149	**ear**	**118**		
body	106	egg	93	**journey**	**67**
book	158	employee	171		
bottle	86	employer	171	**kettle**	**26**
bowl	30	employment	171	key	133
bread	98	envelope	166	kiss	117
breakfast	74			knee	111
bus	59	**face**	**115**	knife	27
button	130	factory	171		
		fence	55	**leg**	**109**
cake	**99**	ferry	62	lenses	134
call	179	field	47	lesson	157
camera	180	finger	110	licence	68
car	58	fish (animal)	50	light	14
card	132	fish (food)	93	lightning	37
carpet	12	floor	12	lips	117
cat	51	flower	53	lorry	63
ceiling	13	fog	39	lunch	74
chair	19	foot	111		
cheese	94	football	150	**magazine**	**163**
chicken	92	forest	46	manager	170
child/children	139	fork	27	mattress	21
				meat	92
				medicine	148

Key Words for Fluency – Pre-intermediate

alphabetical list of words

menu	79	**rain**	**36**	tea	83
milk	94	restaurant	76	teacher	155
minute	182	result	151	telephone	178
mirror	19	rice	100	test	157
moon	35	ring	133	theatre	174
month	182	river	43	throat	117
mountain	46	road	66	thunder	37
moustache	114	room	11	ticket	70
mouth	116			tie	123
muscle	106	**salt**	**103**	toaster	26
museum	174	sand	45	toe	110
		sandwich	98	toilet	23
nail	**110**	scarf	126	tongue	117
neck	119	school	154	tooth	116
newspaper	162	score	151	tour	69
nose	118	sea	42	tourist	69
		seat	71	towel	23
office	**170**	secretary	170	train	61
oil	93	service	78	tree	54
oven	26	sheet	21	trousers	122
		shelf	28		
package	**167**	shirt	122	**umbrella**	**135**
page	159	shoe	127	uniform	125
pan	29	shop	90		
paper	165	shoulders	119	**vegetables**	**95**
parcel	167	show	175	video	181
parent	138	shower	22	virus	147
pasta	100	sink	31		
pen	164	skin	107	**waist**	**108**
pencil	164	sky	34	waiter	77
pet	51	smile	117	waitress	77
petrol	59	snow	38	wall	13
phone	178	sock	126	wallet	132
photo / photograph	180	soldier	173	wardrobe	21
pill	148	spoon	27	washing machine	26
pillow	21	stairs	10	watch	135
play	175	stamp	166	wave	42
plane	60	star	35	wedding	140
plant	52	stitches	149	week	182
plate	30	stomach	107	wife	141
player	151	student	156	wind	39
pocket	130	sugar	102	window	15
police	172	sun	34	wine	85
pot	29	supermarket	91	wrist	109
potatoes	101	sweater	123		
present	143			**x-ray**	**149**
		table	**18**		
queue	**70**	table (restaurant)	79	**year**	**182**
		taxi	62	**zip**	**130**

your own words